THE REFERENCE SHELF   VOLUME 40 NUMBER 2

EAST AFRICA

EDITED BY

WILLIAM P. LINEBERRY

Managing Editor, Foreign Policy Association

THE H. W. WILSON COMPANY
NEW YORK   1968

THE REFERENCE SHELF

The books in this series contain reprints of articles, excerpts from books, and addresses on current issues and social trends in the United States and other countries. There are six separately bound numbers in each volume, all of which are generally published in the same calendar year. One number is a collection of recent speeches; each of the others is devoted to a single subject and gives background information and discussion from various points of view, concluding with a comprehensive bibliography.

Subscribers to the current volume receive the books as issued. The subscription rate is $14 in the United States and Canada ($17 foreign) for a volume of six numbers. Single numbers are $3.50 each in the United States and Canada ($4 foreign).

PREFACE

At a time when the news from Africa seems all bad, and the generally accepted picture is one of a continent torn by the trials of independence and self-rule, a compilation such as this should lend balance and perspective. Racial turmoil, internal strife, economic backsliding and military coups are not the whole story of newly independent Africa's fate. Steady progress, enlightened cooperation, and political tranquillity are in evidence, too—though, regrettably, such matters seldom capture either our attention or the headlines.

East Africa today offers grounds for encouragement. The three nations which are the focus of this compilation—Kenya, Tanzania and Uganda—recently restored their common market and extended their economic cooperation and integration inside a new East African Community. In addition, Kenya and neighboring Somalia have agreed to restore peace and security along their disputed border—and Zambia, Ethiopia, and Somalia have each expressed interest in associating themselves with the newly formed economic community.

In Kenya the legacy of colonialism is being overcome: no one can doubt that the white man in Kenya today fares far better than the black man under *apartheid* in South Africa—a tribute both to the native tolerance of Kenyan Africans and to their willingness to forgive. In Tanzania a new, austere, and distinctly African brand of socialism is emerging which stresses self-help, cooperation, and an end to privilege for the "new class" of bureaucrats that has come to power in so many newly independent African states. Uganda, though saddled with one-man rule and a sluggish economy, is evincing a cooperative spirit toward its neighbors and has thus far avoided the threat of a military takeover.

Undeniably, East Africa has its problems. One-party rule, widespread poverty, and political scandal are as rife there as in much of tropical Africa as a whole. Surrounded by troubled or trouble-making neighbors—Sudan in the north, the Congo in the west, white-ruled Rhodesia, South Africa and Mozambique in the south —Kenya, Tanzania, and Uganda share a precarious stability in a setting fraught with dangers. One can only hope that their example spreads outward before they are themselves engulfed by the turmoil that surrounds them.

This compilation is designed to give the reader an over-all view of East Africa's progress and problems today. The first, introductory, section stakes out the basic setting: newly independent Africa's role in the world, the geography of the area, the historic heritage of cooperation and interdependence in East Africa, and the recent moves toward greater unity. In the second section political close-ups of Kenya, Tanzania, and Uganda since independence are brought into view. Next, the economic prospects and problems facing the three countries are examined. The fourth section explores customs, culture, race, and society in the area. And, in the last section, East Africa's troubled neighbors take the spotlight. The compilation concludes with an American view—that of Under Secretary of State Nicholas deB. Katzenbach—of Africa's future prospects as a whole.

The compiler wishes to thank the authors and publishers who have courteously granted permission for the reprinting of their materials in this book. He is especially indebted to Stephanie Dranoff of Cowles Communications, Inc. for her generous and able assistance in the preparation of the manuscript.

WILLIAM P. LINEBERRY

March 1968

A NOTE TO THE READER

The reader's attention is directed to two other Reference Shelf numbers also dealing with Africa: *The New Nations of West Africa* (Volume 32, Number 2), edited by Robert Theobald and published in 1960, and *North Africa* (Volume 38, Number 5), edited by Ronald Steel and published in 1967.

CONTENTS

III. Economic Problems and Prospects

IV. Race and Society

V. East Africa's Troubled Neighbors

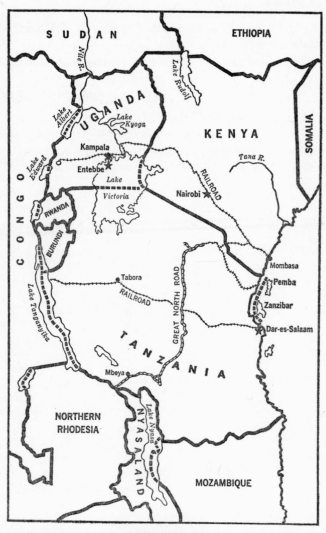

EAST AFRICA

Map from *An East African Federation*, by Carl G. Rosberg, Jr.
Carnegie Endowment for International Peace. New York. '63. Reprinted
by permission.

I. THE SETTING

EDITOR'S INTRODUCTION

The sad fact is that newly independent Africa has yet to make its distinctive mark on the world. One may say, in fact, that far from helping to solve the world's unwieldy bundle of problems Africa's new states have by and large contributed to its bulk. Should we have expected otherwise? Common sense tells us that before tropical Africa can make its contribution to the world it must first find itself.

It is encouraging to note that the new states of East Africa seem to be finding themselves. Kenya, Tanzania, and Uganda—which gained independence from British colonial rule, respectively, in 1963, 1961, and 1962—have weathered the initial uncertainties of self-government and are launched, after some hesitation, upon a course toward greater unity and cooperation. The path before them is far from smooth, the uncertainties many. But while much of Africa today offers cause for pessimism, East Africa is emerging as a source of cautious optimism.

This section is designed to introduce the reader to East Africa—its surroundings, its background, and its prospects. In the first article a political scientist at Western Reserve University sets the stage with a discussion of newly independent Africa's emerging role in the world. The reader will note the pressures working on East Africa at this time of uncertainty. In the second article a geographer intimately acquainted with the East African landscape, Paul Fordham, introduces us to the beauty and variety, both human and geographic, of this part of the world.

The last three articles of this section deal with the prospects for regional cooperation, toward which East Africa has recently made significant strides. In the first of these, two scholars writing for the Carnegie Endowment for International Peace trace the history of regional cooperation and integration down to the time of independence. The second article describes the post-independence moves away from unity toward fragmentation and notes the prospects for new arrangements and wider cooperation. In the last article of this section—a dispatch from the New York *Times*—a "happy ending" is proffered. The dispatch describes the decision taken December 1, 1967, by Kenya, Tanzania, and Uganda to form an East African Community.

AFRICA IN THE WORLD ARENA [1]

For most of the world's new states, foreign policy is of secondary importance. Of necessity domestic considerations take precedence. Although the foreign policies of the new states of Africa cannot be understood exclusively in terms of internal affairs, they cannot be understood at all if the internal milieu is ignored. This is not strictly a characteristic of new states, but, with them, its manifestations are more obvious. First, the fragility of the new states and nations is all too evident. They lack historical sanction; their legitimacy is constantly brought into question; their future existence is subject to doubt. Moreover, the governments are even more tenuous than the states themselves.

In such a context, foreign policy serves numerous purposes. It can be a cohesive element projecting preindependence movements into postcolonial times, thus preserving the fragile unity forged in the anticolonial struggle. It can accentuate the identity of the state in a community of nation-states. It can enhance the prestige of the national leader at home and reduce the effectiveness of his opposition. It can be used as a rationale for repressive domestic policies. It can help the struggle for greater independence and economic development and thereby reduce foreign influences on its domestic life.

The chief foreign policy concern of Africa has been, and is, the anticolonial struggle. East-West competition touches on this issue, but to Africans it is not their primary interest. In short, the cold war is important to African governments only to the extent that it affects and can be used for their own ends—the prompt elimination

[1] From article by Kenneth W. Grundy, associate professor of political science, Western Reserve University. *Current History.* 52:129-35+. Mr. '67. Reprinted by permission.

of colonial and settler governments in Africa and the economic and political development of their states.

An American Perspective

Still, from an American perspective, there is some utility in viewing Africa in an East-West framework. This, after all, has been the chief tenet of United States international policy for over twenty years and it still serves as a touchstone of popular and official international discussion. If such a view somewhat distorts reality, if it imputes to Africans goals and policies they never intended, that is our error. It is not entirely fortuitous that Africa entered the international community during the East-West rivalry; the modified cold war offers Africa's statemen promise as well as problems.

Since the famous Bandung Conference of Afro-Asian states in 1955, the dominant governmental attitude of the independent African states toward the Western and Communist alliance systems has been one of nonalignment. Although there have been different varieties and interpretations of the concept, it represents for the nonwhite, non-Western, ex-colonial states of Africa and Asia a common approach to the dangers of a world divided into two inexorably hostile camps—or so it seemed in the 1950's. Their chief objectives have been to achieve legal independence and to solidify economic and political independence.

In spite of the different policy interpretations of nonalignment, there has been an underlying consensus among its proponents regarding its basic tenets. Disagreement seems to arise about matters of ideological orientation and subsequent policy decisions. For example, there is common agreement that, although they wish to be nonaligned, the African states are not neutral, not insensitive, to the moral issues involved in the East-West conflict. Nonalignment does not mean that they are detached, uncommitted, unwilling to take sides in what they regard to be matters of ethical import. African neutralists see no virtue in steering a middle course equidistant between East and West. Rather, they have values and they are fully prepared to take sides on given issues. They merely wish to maintain diplomatic maneuverability and freedom of choice.

What they want is not so much nonalignment for its own sake, but nonalignment because it facilitates and is a manifestation of the political freedom a truly sovereign and independent state expects. If, as a matter of choice arising out of several live alternatives, a professedly nonaligned state's policy should happen to coincide closely with one or the other of the cold war rivals, then that state would probably maintain that it was still fundamentally nonaligned. While free choice for economically and militarily weak and dependent states may be an ideal rather than a reality, its impact as a goal for which they strive cannot be emphasized too much. What the advocates of nonalignment oppose is *permanent* or *obligatory* diplomatic and military identification with the great powers.

The themes and the statements about nonalignment by leaders of the different African states may have much in common. But their actual relations with the United States, the U.S.S.R., and the former metropoles do not. One recent study attempts to devise a technique to measure alignment and to validate the measurements by polling a selection of area specialists and international relations generalists. Each was asked to rank 119 countries on an alignment scale. Alignment scores indicated that, of any geographical area, Africa ranked farthest from the United States. Yet it still fell about half-way between two designations: "neutral with leanings toward U.S.," and "neutral or aligned with third party." No African state fell among the twenty states regarded as most aligned with the United States. On the other hand, six were numbered among those closest to the Soviet Union: Zanzibar, Ghana, Rwanda, United Arab Republic, Algeria and Guinea. Significantly, if in the African framework one is searching for ties with the West, France and not the United States serves as the pole of attraction for states such as Chad, Dahomey, Gabon, Ivory Coast, Malagasy, Niger and Togo.

The alignment scores (although not the techniques) have been somewhat outdated by developments in Africa. The coups in Algeria (June 19, 1965) and Ghana (Februay 24, 1966) have removed these states from the Russian sphere of influence. The union of Zanzibar and Tanganyika (April 23, 1964) withdrew Zanzibar as an autonomous actor in international politics, although the union coincided with President Julius Nyerere's increasing criticisms of the West, particularly the United States. Mali continues to present an image of hostility to the West—one occasionally in accord with Communist positions—although in actual policy it is more cir-cumspect and appears to be genuinely nonaligned. Congo (Brazzaville) and Burundi have evidenced a close attachment to the Chinese People's Republic. What this means is that Africa is still extremely fluid. Changes in government and single events can alter postures that have not had an opportunity to harden.

The United States and Africa

American participation in the Stanleyville rescue of November 1964 stands as a landmark in United States-African relations. On the surface this action in the Congo (Leopoldville—now known as Kinshasa) could be regarded as the nadir of American policy in Africa. The generally favorable image fostered by foreign assistance and the sympathetic policy of the Kennedy administration was shattered by American-British-Belgian cooperation in an overtly military operation. Throughout the continent, radical and moderate governments joined the chorus of condemnation, which lasted well into 1965.

Washington's unfortunate identification with and support of the Moise Tshombe regime in the Congo beginning in July 1964 pre-ceded the Stanleyville rescue. United States relations with several of the Congo's neighbors, Congo (Brazzaville), Sudan and Tanzania, took a turn for the worse. Each of these states gave encouragement, sanctuary, and material assistance to the Stanley-ville rebel government. Thus, their policies clashed with the aims and activities of the United States. In each state, United States charges of outside interference in Congolese domestic affairs pre-cipitated their countercharges of United States meddling in their internal affairs.

The present status of relations with the Sudan is good; with Tanzania, strained; with Congo (Brazzaville), poor. In August 1965 the United States withdrew its diplomatic and consular representa-tives from Brazzaville, because of apparently calculated harassment, and normal representation has not been resumed.

U.S.-Tanzanian Friction

The Tanzanian situation is a little more complicated. On November 12, 1964, Tanzanian Minister of External Affairs Oscar Kambona denounced an alleged plot to subvert his government. Photostats of three letters were published in the ruling party press purporting to show that the United States had plotted with Great Britain to use Portuguese and South African mercenaries to attack strategic points in Tanzania. The United States ambassador immediately denied the charges and labeled the documents "clumsy forgeries." Later, the Tanzanian government turned them over to the United States embassy whose experts scrutinized them and concurred in the ambassador's appraisal. This was followed by the expulsion of two American diplomats in January 1965. They had been accused of "subversive activities," in this instance a case of mistaken interpretation of a monitored telephone conversation. After American denials, Washington countered by expelling a Tanzanian diplomat. Ultimately, both governments recalled their ambassadors.

Although the Tanzanian government never did issue an explanation of the initial charges or join with the United States in an examination of the facts, neither side wished to see the situation worsen. President Nyerere was not entirely in agreement with his foreign minister and sought an improvement in relations. The American ambassador returned to Dar es Salaam by June 1965, and the Tanzanian embassy in Washington was reopened in October.

Thus, in Africa, the United States sometimes finds itself regarded as a status quo (and sometimes reactionary) force too closely identified with the colonial and ex-colonial and the white settler regimes, and in some instances (and with some justification) of trying to fill the vacuum left by the departing European colonialists. On the other hand, there are other countries where the United States has seen an encouraging improvement in relations, largely because of domestic changes, or Chinese Communist or Soviet Union blunders. Kenya, Ghana and Algeria come to mind. The recent military coups in Algeria and Ghana were greeted with relief in Washington. In the past the United States usually waited several weeks before recognizing new military governments, to avoid the impression that it was encouraging or was involved in military coups. In the case of Ghana the United States waited only one week.

What stands out, however, is the over-all decline of official American interest in Africa and an increasing willingness to let Africans solve their own problems, provided there is no interference from other "radical" states either in Africa or abroad. Over the past two or three years the United States has become preoccupied with the war in Vietnam. As a result, African problems (with the exception of headline issues and a growing business investment in selected areas) have been avoided or ignored. United States economic assistance to Africa has declined steadily since 1962. Likewise, congressional interest and time devoted to Africa has diminished since about the same time. Moreover, in recent sessions, Congress has grown increasingly critical of black Africa and more sympathetic to settler Africa. Chances are this tendency will continue in the Ninetieth Congress. Crudely put, Africa is not central to the concerns of American policy-makers and congressmen.

The Communist World and Africa

At a time when United States involvement in African affairs seems to be lessening, Soviet and Chinese involvement is likewise changing. Apparently, the Soviet Union is in the process of rethinking its role in Africa. Aid from Soviet bloc countries has not increased lately, and in states where they formerly exercised considerable influence (Algeria, Ghana, Guinea and Mali), some Communists have been asked to leave and others have voluntarily diminished their presence. The Soviet Union did not fare especially well in Guinea during the period of her greatest concentration of effort and money (1958-1962), nor did its close ties with other states pay the kind of political dividends her leaders had come to expect. From a Soviet standpoint Africans have become unmanageable— more independent, more perceptive, and more sensitive than originally supposed. The result has been a lot of talk from the Kremlin recently, but not much real revolutionary activity in Africa proper. The Soviet Union seems to have shifted gears, emphasizing diplomacy and normal channels of contact rather than subversion and ideological purity.

One obvious problem confronting the Soviet Union has been the military coups in Algeria and Ghana. The other military coups in Africa fit rather easily into the framework of the Soviet conception of neocolonialism and popular unrest in nominally independent states. But in Soviet parlance, Ghana and Algeria—along with Guinea, Mali, and the U.A.R. [United Arab Republic, i.e. Egypt]— were closest to being "progressive," antiimperialist, antifeudalist, and noncapitalist "national democracies." In spite of hints in the Russian press about "imperialist agents" behind the coups, the comparative ease of takeover has led the Soviets to realize that the regimes they backed were not so popular as previously supposed. In discussions of Africa and the third world at the twenty-third party congress in March 1966, speakers seemed to indicate that the U.S.S.R. was truly upset by the turn of events in Ghana. As a result of the ensuing confusion, a decline in doctrinal pronouncement on Africa is discernible. Soviet spokesmen are now forced to develop a more flexible and pragmatic substitute for what has proven to be the bankrupt doctrine of "national democracy."

There are several possible explanations for these changes. It may be that Chinese and American influence in Africa has fallen off, thus making it possible for the Russians to cut back without losing touch. After all, they have constructed a rather solid diplomatic base in Africa over the years. It may be that the Africans are becoming more wary of Soviet techniques and propaganda. Perhaps the Soviets are genuinely perplexed as to how to approach Africa, and they may have decided to temporize and study the matter, hoping their rivals may stumble and fall, enabling them to step in effectively. An October 1965 article from *Pravda* warns of this frustration when it suggests that "the best way to fulfill our internationalist duty to the working people of the entire world is the successful construction of socialism and communism." Although this by no means presages a voluntary isolation of the Soviet Union in the world, it does smack of Joseph Stalin's "socialism in one country" and the international implications of that policy. Whatever the reasons, it appears that the Soviet Union is undergoing some serious rethinking on the whole problem of how best to promote its interests in the underdeveloped world.

Peking's Influence Dwindling

Lately, Africa's politicians have been even less hospitable to Chinese Communists than to Americans or Russians. Chinese Premier Chou En-lai's often quoted remark that "Africa is ripe for revolution" has come to haunt him. Yet this slogan fits easily into China's over-all view of Africa in the world revolution. To the Chinese, legal independence does not necessarily mean that a state enjoys real political and economic independence. Africa, like China before it, must be prepared for a long struggle. Contemporary Africa, thus, can be compared to China in the early twentieth century. Some African states are relatively free from foreign influence, and some are effectively ruled from abroad. It is, therefore, neocolonialism and its vanguard, the United States, that must be eliminated from Africa. The protracted revolution is to follow the format of Chinese Defense Minister Lin Piao's 1965 article on the struggle between the "world countryside" (the underdeveloped states) and the "world cities" (the "have" countries). To this end, the Chinese have trained guerrillas, bribed politicians, set up front organizations, extended some foreign aid and entertained students and statesmen from Africa. A mark of China's success was that, by 1965, eighteen of thirty-six African states had extended diplomatic recognition to the Chinese People's Republic (C.P.R.). But the Chinese are learning, as did the Americans and Russians, that Africans will not easily surrender independence.

When Chou En-lai first visited Africa (December 1963 to February 1964), China's prospects in Africa looked good. But recently it seems to have lost some of its appeal. Events involving Africa, both internal and international, have been strongly unfavorable to China's cause. In Algeria, Burundi, Central African Republic, the Congo (Kinshasa), Dahomey, Ghana, Kenya, Mali, Somalia, and Tanzania, it has seen its presence decline. The only country where the C.P.R. appears to have gained markedly in influence is Congo (Brazzaville). Although, for Africa's revolutionaries, China is still the shining standard for a peasant-based revolution, revolutionary Africans are themselves losing favor and influence. The indefinite postponement of the Asian-African Conference scheduled for August 1965 in Algiers was an additional blow to Peking's penetration in Africa.

Africa's statesmen, seemingly, began to realize that a call to revolution for Africa's masses would be directed at *their* own governments. China's recent failures (and this is by no means an irreversible trend) can be attributed to the basic incompatibility between China's foreign policy objectives (and particularly its conception of the fundamentals of the protracted world revolution) and the interests and aspirations of Africa's governing elites.

African Unity: Ideal and Reality

African unity is closely related to nonalignment. At its base is a desire to assure the independence of Africa and to extend Africa's influence in world affairs. By uniting the continent, Africans see economic advantage, greater security, more prestige, and increased opportunity to transform international power relationships. The basic question regarding African unity is not, "Shall we have unity?" but rather, "How shall unity be brought about and how rapidly?" A question deferred until later but embedded in all discussions is, "Who shall lead a united Africa?"

Virtually every African politician has repeatedly asserted his devotion to the ideal of pan-African unity. At the crux of the debate are the mechanics and extent of unification. There are two major approaches: one is political, the other is economic. Versions of these approaches differ as to geographical coverage—continental, sub-Saharan, or regional. But central to each is the unchallengeable fact that, before unity can be achieved, those in positions of authority must be convinced that their interests will be served by radically altering the established patterns of intra-African relations. So far, there has been no indication that a concerted willingness to change exists, despite the almost constant demand for greater cooperation and unity.

Although the climate of sentiment sympathetic to demands for unity appears to have existed prior to the overthrow of President

Kwame Nkrumah of Ghana—once the chief spokesman for continent-wide political unification—the leaders of most states, for many reasons, have not made the sacrifices necessary to achieve unity. The Organization of African Unity (OAU) does not appear to constitute the kind of unity which Africans advocate. Some would contend that Nkrumah's overthrow will make unity more difficult; others that with Nkrumah out of the picture the reluctance to unify will disappear. Unity is still a long way off, and for those wary of broad-ranging unification schemes, Nkrumah's presence or absence makes little difference.

Regardless of personalities, unity opens a Pandora's box of imponderables. The recent history of the OAU illustrates these ongoing problems. Temporarily at least, ideological and personal animosities were overcome and the general aura of compromise and cooperation was institutionalized when the OAU was created at Addis Ababa in 1963. The critical issues which had divided the Casablanca and Monrovia groups—the independence of Algeria and the civil war in the Congo—had been settled (the latter superficially) so that differences could be papered over. Intra-African relations were never again to be quite the same. When the old rivalries reemerged, they were subsumed under the institutional framework of the OAU. Still, the survival of the OAU was in question.

Before the second OAU summit could convene in Cairo in mid-July 1964, the Congo crisis flared again and schisms so near the surface opened. In July 1964 Moise Tshombe was named prime minister of the Congo (Kinshasa) and was promptly banned from attending the Cairo summit. The fighting in the Congo's eastern provinces grew in intensity. One group of states claimed its duty was to assist the rebels in the name of antineocolonialism. Another group rejected subversion and external (although African) interference in the domestic affairs of a sovereign state. Algeria, Ghana and the United Arab Republic (U.A.R.) once again openly sought the destruction of an African government that they regarded as neocolonialist. In retaliation, the four "moderate" French-speaking states (led by Ivory Coast) created the Organisation Commune Africaine et Malgache (OCAM) early in 1965, to thwart subversive activities and to reintegrate the Congolese government into African diplomatic life. Africa once more was rent by fundamental ideological divisions.

Impact of Rhodesia's UDI

These became evident at the October 1965 OAU summit meeting in Accra. For some time preceding the conference there was a question whether or not it would be convened. Although the Congo rebellion had been subdued but not extinguished, several heads of state maintained that as long as Nkrumah harbored political refugees from their countries and trained them in subversion, they would not go to Accra. Consequently, eight states were unrepresented at Accra—the OCAM four (Ivory Coast, Dahomey, Niger, Upper Volta), plus Chad, Gabon, Malagasy and Togo. The Accra summit, though unproductive, was not a total loss. The Congo issue no longer plagued the OAU (President Joseph Kasavubu had dismissed Tshombe one week earlier). Instead, the Rhodesian crisis helped supply a sense of urgency and cooperation. Not knowing precisely what course the Rhodesian regime of Ian Smith would take, the heads of state found little difficulty reaching agreement condemning a possible unilateral declaration of independence (UDI). The resolution represented a victory for the "moderates." Despite the absence of the main complainants, the heads of state also agreed "not to tolerate . . . any subversion originating in our countries against another Member State" of the OAU.

As for Nkrumah's advocacy of union government, consideration of his toned-down proposal to create an executive council as the "executive arm" for the heads-of-state assembly was postponed until the meeting scheduled for 1966 in Addis Ababa. Ethiopia's Emperor Haile Selassie offered a substitute resolution to establish a committee to study Nkrumah's proposal and, although it received 18 votes for to 5 against, it failed to get the requisite 24 votes (two thirds of the members) to carry.

Despite these difficulties, there are some who believe that the Accra summit "strengthened" the OAU. The very fact that it was actually held was cause for jubilation in some quarters. For the first time, the heads-of-state assembly dispensed with its set procedure of public speeches. Rather, plenary debates were conducted in closed session, with more of the give and take so necessary for genuine compromise. But, at best, the Accra summit was an exercise in cooperation and compromise on foreign policy matters. It cannot be regarded as an exhibition of unity along the lines the activists envision.

Shortly afterwards, on November 12, 1965, the Smith government announced UDI for Rhodesia. Foreign ministers and defense ministers of thirty-five OAU states (Gambia was absent) met in Addis Ababa to decide how to proceed. In an emotional atmosphere it was resolved unanimously (although with some difficulty) that, if Great Britain did not crush the Rhodesian rebellion by December 15 (less than two weeks away), all OAU members would break off diplomatic relations with Britain. The results were disastrous. The presidents of Tunisia and Upper Volta publicly disavowed their foreign ministers' decisions. A statement by the Nigerian foreign minister was also officially corrected. Most other members reserved the right to interpret the resolution flexibly. Between December 15 and 19, only nine states broke with Britain—Ghana and Tanzania (of the Commonwealth), and Algeria, Congo (Brazzaville), Guinea, Mali, Mauritania, Sudan and the U.A.R. By taking hasty action without consulting their capitals, the ministers had seriously weakened the credibility of the organization. Further dissension surfaced at the sixth ordinary session of the OAU Council of Ministers (February 28 to March 6, 1966) where eight of the thirty-six members walked out in protest. The 1966 summit conference at Addis Ababa in November deepened the splits. The dispute between Ghana and Guinea dominated the proceedings and it was only Rhodesia's continued defiance of the Africans that held the conference together.

The collective approach to Africa's problems is not solidly ingrained. The OAU continues to exist, but its record is checkered. The possibility of a return to the old bloc politics of the 1960-1963 period is real and might develop within the context of the OAU itself. Few Africans wish to see the disappearance of the OAU. But its future depends primarily on the nature of the issues that arise. If bilateral, nonideological intra-African issues crop up, they may be subject to resolution or mitigation. But ideological issues arouse more widespread interest and could possibly present the OAU with divisive pressures the African states and the OAU would be unable to handle. Clearly, African unity is fragile. The dreams of the continent are no closer to fulfillment than they were in 1963.

Independent Politics

It remains clear that African states jealously guard their independence, limited as it may be, against all challenges. In the three-cornered East-West competition, no power has been able to dominate the continent, though the West and particularly the ex-colonial powers seem to have been and continue to be the most successful in exerting influence.

Further, this is not a simple three-cornered game. The Africans are themselves acting as well as being acted upon. Moreover, there is no real "balancing" of influence. Rather, the European powers and increasingly the United States have an advantage. Peking and Moscow are hardly of the same magnitude except—and this is an important exception from an American perspective—in a few selected countries. What is really amazing is that, in spite of their almost total economic dependence on the West, some African states have managed to take rather independent international courses. If unity could be fostered or if new, more powerful groupings developed, Africans would be in an even better position to resist external pressures and conduct more independent foreign policies.

EAST AFRICA—AN OVERVIEW [2]

East Africa is a land of great variety; in physical features, climate, human types, economic development, and political evolution alike. There are few places on the earth's surface where, in the space of a few hundred miles, you can experience such a range of contrasts. You can pass from high mountain snows to the deepest lake-filled troughs lined with tropical vegetation; from the invigorating climate of the highland areas to the dusty heat of the rift valley floors, or from bustling modern cities to a countryside

[2] From *Geography of African Affairs*, by Paul Fordham, principal of the College of Social Studies at Kikuyu, Kenya. Penguin. Baltimore. '65. p 181-94. Reprinted by permission.

still largely devoted to subsistence agriculture. It would, moreover, be false to make a firm distinction between developed towns and an underdeveloped countryside. There are great differences between one area and another. Particularly in Kenya, you can move from a fully commercial agriculture to the poorest subsistence farming or from fertile volcanic soils, like those round Kilimanjaro in Tanganyika [now Tanzania], to the poor and eroded pastures of the Masai on the floor and margins of the rift valley. Finally, there are in East Africa all the clashes of tribal and racial interests present in other parts of the continent and great contrasts in the types of state which have emerged from the race to independence.

These diverse environments and their many difficult problems have been given a certain unity by two facts, one physical and the other political.

Away from the coast, the encircling arms of the eastern and western rift valley systems are a unique feature of the African physical scene and are responsible for many of the region's physical and human contrasts. The western rift mountains and lakes cut East Africa off from the Congo Basin and from Northern Rhodesia [now Zambia], while the eastern and western rift highlands alike contain fertile volcanic soils and some of Africa's highest population densities. In between the two arms the plateau surface centers on the fertile, well-watered and thickly populated Lake Victoria depression.

Politically, with the exception of Ruanda [Rwanda] and Burundi, all the territories have been under British rule and use English as an official language. [Kenya and Tanzania also use Swahili.] Most of Kenya was a crown colony, except the coastal strip which was a protectorate; Uganda and Zanzibar were protectorates, while Tanganyika has been administered by Britain under UN trusteeship. Both Tanganyika and Ruanda Burundi were German colonies in the years before the First World War but Belgium became the administering power for the latter country and tended, until recently, to make little distinction between Ruanda/Burundi and the colony of Congo. The British territories have enjoyed common tariff arrangements and certain common services, like railways, administered by the EACSO [East African Common Services Organization, formerly the East African High Commission]. How much of these common services and arrangements will be preserved after the withdrawal of British power is one of the important questions to be settled in the immediate future.

Land and Climate

East Africa may conveniently be divided into five natural regions which, as so often throughout the continent, cut right across the political boundaries.

The coastal fringe, varying in width from ten to forty miles, has an equatorial climate with abundant though not excessive rain and accompanying tropical vegetation. This part of East Africa has had centuries of contact with the outside world, contact which is reflected in the cosmopolitan racial, cultural, and architectural character of the cities of the coast.

Prior to the coming of British and German rule the coast was controlled by the Sultan of Zanzibar. Germany bought the Tanganyika coast for £200,000 in 1890, but the Kenya coast became a protectorate over which the Sultan of Zanzibar still had some claim until 1963.

The coastal hinterland, for the most part dry and uninviting, cuts off the coast from the great population centers of the interior. Whereas the coast has long been known to the outside world the inland areas were only well known towards the end of the nineteenth century. In Kenya the zone is one of semidesert and in most of the long rail haul from Mombasa to Nairobi (about three hundred miles) there are few people and little economic activity. This dry zone becomes more marked as you move northwards in Kenya and the whole northern half of the country is semidesert or desert. In Tanganyika the coastal hinterland is better watered and inland from Tanga contains the extensive sisal estates which are the country's principal source of developed wealth.

The highlands of the eastern rift, mainly over five thousand feet, are a discontinuous zone with many natural advantages of soil and climate. Temperatures are comfortably modified by the altitude, the soils are deep and, like most volcanic soils, have a valuable reserve of natural fertility when not abused. The climate and the crops grown tend to vary with altitude rather than with season or latitude and there may be great variety within a small area. In the Kenya highlands, for example, you can see wheat, oats, barley, pyrethrum, tea, coffee, and pineapples all flourishing within a few miles of each other.

The western rift highlands of Ruanda, Burundi and Western Uganda are less well known and, because of their distance from the sea, less developed. They are, however, naturally fertile and support a dense African population. Ruanda and Burundi have nearly five million people (1960), more than the whole of Angola.

The interior plateau, lying between the two rift systems and about four thousand feet above sea level, is largely arid or semiarid bush country, much of it infested with tsetse fly. The chief exception to the general aridity is the land on the margins of Lake Victoria. The lake has considerable local influence in producing a climate with a well-distributed rainfall. As a result, the Nyanza province of Kenya, the southern half of Uganda and, to a smaller extent, the lake shores of Tanganyika are able to support a dense and relatively prosperous African population.

Land: A Basic Necessity

It will already be evident from this description that there are considerable areas of East Africa too dry for successful farming. The East Africa Royal Commission estimated that a fair prospect of receiving twenty inches of rain a year was necessary for successful ranching and a fair prospect of thirty inches of rain a year was necessary for successful arable farming. Considerable areas do not measure up to these standards. In addition, much land which might otherwise be suitable for cattle is infested with tsetse fly. Some 10 per cent of Kenya, 32 per cent of Uganda, and 60 per cent of Tanganyika is tsetse infested. . . .

Areas which have both a poor chance of thirty inches of rain and tsetse infestation are useless for both arable farming and cattle ranching. Areas with less than twenty inches are also useless without irrigation. Small wonder that the people of East Africa are scattered in islands of high density in those areas which are more favorable to human activity.

Contrasts between the fertile and the infertile, the well-watered and the arid, are so great in East Africa that land hunger and competition for land are pressing problems, especially in Kenya. The position was summed up by the East Africa Royal Commission in 1955 as follows:

> If a panorama picture could be taken slowly, and over a period, of the way people are living in East Africa, the most striking feature of it would be a restless anxiety to obtain and hold on to the land. Land is still, for the vast majority, a basic necessity from which each family derives its own food by its own physical effort. Where this can be done with the least effort for the greatest result, people have tended to collect and tend to want to stay. This tendency has been accentuated by the difficulty of penetrating the unknown where tsetse and lack of water have proved insurmountable obstacles, and by the hazards of uncertain rainfall over such a large part of the region. Thus the places where good rainfall, good soil, water and grazing are most easily obtained, the risks of human and animal disease most easily avoided, are in the greatest demand. As population has increased—and this has generally been greatest in these most favorable localities—so has pressure increased in two directions, outwards, so as to get more land if possible and to obtain as fertile land as possible, and inwards, towards a more devastating use of the land itself. The inward pressure, under contemporary systems of land usage, is affecting production from the soil adversely. This is the most serious aspect of the land problem. The outward pressure results in conflict wherever fertile land is short. . . .

The People

Contrasts in the land and the distribution of population are paralleled by contrasts in the people themselves. Not only are there several immigrant groups to contend with—notably the Europeans, Asians, and Arabs—but the differences between the African tribes in language and political outlook are just as important in some areas.

East Africa is the meeting point for all the continent's major linguistic groups. Even the "click" languages [characteristic of southern Africa] are represented in central Tanganyika. The three groups of greatest importance are the Nilotic, the Nilo-Hamitic, and the Bantu, and of these the latter are by far the most important. Of the tribes whose numbers are around the million mark only the Luo are a non-Bantu people.

The political importance of tribal differences varies greatly in the three territories. Tribalism appears to be unimportant in Tanganyika, important in the case of one major tribe in Uganda, and, immediately prior to independence, seemed a seriously divisive factor in Kenya.

In Tanganyika there are between 80 and 120 tribal groups, none of whom is numerically anywhere near the million mark except the Sukuma of the southern shores of Lake Victoria. Unlike some of the important tribes of Kenya and Uganda, the geographical situation of the Sukuma makes them remote from the capital city and center of political activity. Partly for this reason, there has never been any question or fear of Sukuma political domination as there is of Baganda domination in Uganda or Kikuyu and Luo domination in Kenya. While the ten largest tribes of Kenya make up between 80 and 90 per cent of the population, in Tanganyika the fourteen biggest tribes make up only just over half the population.

Tribalism in Tanganyika has also been made less important by the use of Swahili as the language of instruction in schools, whereas in Kenya and Uganda the various vernacular tongues have been given greater encouragement; there are also fewer trained and educated leaders in Tanganyika than the other two territories and therefore less competition for the top political jobs.

Whatever the reasons, Tanganyika on the verge of independence presented a remarkable picture of political unity. In the elections of 1960 no fewer than fifty-eight seats went to unopposed candidates of TANU [Tanganyika African National Union], an achievement paralleled only in those countries where no effective opposition is allowed to exist. This is not to say that opposition will not develop, even of a regional kind. The fact that Tanganyika's populous and productive areas are scattered around its periphery might well lead to the emergence of regional discontent. This is made the more likely by the country's great size and poor communications. At present, however, we have the prospect of a strong central government in independent Tanganyika with a ruling party which now has all parliamentary seats and has made all other parties illegal.

Uganda and Its Tribes

The situation is quite otherwise in Uganda, where the tribal loyalties and political acumen of the leaders of Buganda have produced a federal constitution for the independence of Uganda in 1962.

The Ganda number close on a million people and are numerically the largest tribe in Uganda. Moreover, their geographically central position places them at the center of economic and political power. The capital city and seat of government are in Buganda, the country's road system radiates out from Buganda and the comparative wealth of the Ganda people has brought them greater educational and job opportunities than other tribes. The average money income per head of Africans in central Buganda is nearly ten times as great as in parts of the western province and over twice as much as that in most other parts of the country.

Buganda's position of wealth and influence, which is due in part to this favorable geographical situation, has also been strengthened by British colonial policy.

When a British protectorate was established in 1900 it was convenient for Britain to control the country through the existing native administration. The agreement between Britain and the Kabaka's government not only confirmed the authority of that government but gave it a status far above that of the surrounding tribes. More than this, the Ganda were rewarded for their loyalty by British recognition of the annexation of territory from the less cooperative Nyoro. This annexation has given rise to the present "lost counties" dispute.

The claims of Bunyoro extend to five of the northern counties of Buganda and parts of two others, all of them claimed on historical grounds as once forming part of the lands of the Nyoro people. The dispute really centers on the three northwestern counties in two of which (Buyaga and Bugangazzi) the Nyoro form an overwhelming majority of the population. For some decades prior to British rule Buganda had been expanding at the expense of Bunyoro so that two or three of the counties would probably have passed to Buganda without British intervention. It is doubtful, however, whether Buganda would have been able to acquire Buyaga and Bugangazzi when it did without British help.

The strength of the feelings aroused by this dispute, not only between the main contestants but among the other tribes of Uganda, is a measure of the suspicions of some other tribes of Buganda's intentions.

> There is . . . a distinct danger that the dispute over the "lost counties" might become a *casus belli* involving other parts of Uganda. Bunyoro has strong traditional connections with the tribes of the northern province, which in general are hostile to Buganda's pretensions. It is possible that the north would support Bunyoro against Buganda and that civil war would result. [Great Britain. Uganda Relationships Commission. Munster report, 1961.]

Buganda is also suspicious in her turn of the infiltration of other tribes into Buganda. The 1959 census showed no less than 47 per cent of the population of the province to be natives of other areas. African immigrants have poured into Buganda in the last forty years in response to the greater economic opportunities existing there. They come from Ruanda, Burundi, and Tanganyika as well as other parts of Uganda and work as unskilled laborers on various construction works, non-African industrial enterprises and, for the Ganda themselves, on the land. Many return home but, as with immigrant groups the world over, an increasing proportion will stay. The birth rate of many of the immigrant tribes is higher than that of the Ganda and it will not be long, at present rates of increase and immigration, before the Ganda are a minority in their own country.

The new federal constitution safeguards the position of Ganda traditional institutions which might have been threatened by immigration and by modern political parties voted into power by the other provinces. And it places Buganda in an even stronger political position than before. It may, however, effectively disfranchise the members of immigrant tribes in Buganda. Certainly a great deal of tribal suspicion will continue to exist. The new constitution is, nevertheless, an expression on all sides of an intention to cooperate. Without such cooperation the future would be bleak indeed. [The election of the Kabaka of Buganda as President of Uganda (1963) has reduced tension between Buganda and the rest of the country.]

The Tribes of Kenya

In Kenya, the larger and economically more advanced tribes—notably the Kikuyu and the Luo—tended to support the party which demanded strong central government (KANU) [Kenya African National Union]. Many of the smaller tribes tended to support the party of "democratic regionalism" (KADU) [Kenya African Democratic Union]. Kenya's main concentrations of population are in three widely separated centers, the Mombasa district, the highlands near Nairobi (the home of the Kikuyu) and Nyanza province (the home of the Luo and others). Each area has different languages, tribes, and economic problems. It would in any case be difficult to weld them into a cohesive political whole. [Such a government has emerged since independence and has succeeded in reducing regional opposition to the minimum necessary for effective cohesion. It has recently achieved a one-party system by agreement. The independence constitution of 1963 divided the country into seven regions and the Nairobi area. One region (the North East) is claimed by Somalia as part of "Greater Somalia." The majority of the people of this region are Somalis (as is the case with the Ogaden of Ethiopia). "Shifta" bandits from Somalia have been an increasing terrorist menace to North East Kenya in recent years.]

The Europeans in Kenya number some 66,000 people or about one in one hundred of the total population. Although they nearly doubled their numbers between 1950 and 1960, they no longer control Kenya's political life and their future is uncertain. [For a more recent assessment of how they are faring, see Section IV, below.] As elsewhere in East Africa, most of them live in the towns, especially Nairobi, and it is a myth to think of them as mainly settlers on the land.

The myth had some substance in the early days of white settlement. Europeans were brought in to farm on the Kenya highlands as a direct result of the building of the Uganda railway, which reached the site of modern Nairobi in 1899 and Kisumu in 1901. The railway had been built to reach the strategic headwaters of the Nile, to open up Uganda to legitimate trade, and to provide support for the Christian missions there. It was, however, a costly undertaking in both lives and money and, partly in order to make it pay, attention was soon directed to developing the highland areas of Kenya through which the railway passed. Under the stimulus provided by the enthusiasm of Lord Delamere and others, European farmers were encouraged to take up land on favorable terms from 1902 onwards and again, under special schemes for ex-servicemen, after the two world wars.

It has always been a small community—growing from just over five thousand in 1914 to nearly seventeen thousand in 1931. In 1931 the largest occupational group was still in agriculture but was already being overtaken by government service and commerce. In 1948, out of the total "gainfully employed" population, only 23 per cent were in agriculture and fishing. Government service, commerce, the professions and clerical occupations together accounted for over 62 per cent of the European population.

Nevertheless, in spite of the small numbers of people involved in farming, the land question has continued to be of immense importance in Kenya politics. Alienation of the former "white highlands" formed the basis of race segregation in Kenya, just as the Land Apportionment Act still does in Southern Rhodesia. It made Nairobi primarily a non-African town and squeezed the Kikuyu between two sectors of European land, into their increasingly overcrowded reserve. It helped to sustain the Mau Mau rebellion and has resulted in exceedingly uneven economic development. Much money and skill has been put into the land in the European areas while only recently has much money and effort been devoted to improving the African areas.

The Asian Community

In Tanganyika about 15 per cent of Europeans are in agriculture but their diverse ethnic origins (Greeks, Germans, and English among others), their peripheral location and their remoteness from the political and commercial capital of the country have combined to reduce their political influence. In Uganda only a handful of Europeans are planters, most of the rest of them being employed in government and other service occupations.

The Asian community has been established in East Africa for longer than many of the African tribes themselves. The myth of the Kenya Europeans as largely "settlers" is paralleled by the myth of Asians as largely descended from laborers brought in to build the Uganda railway. Arab traders have been on the coast for close on two thousand years and Indians have probably been there for nearly as long. It would indeed be surprising if they had not.

The geographical unity of the Indian Ocean, and the ancient navigation routes across it based on regularly changing monsoon winds, means that the East African coast has always provided bases for the brisk trading activities of the area. As elsewhere in Africa, the settlements remained coastal until the nineteenth century, but the enterprise and civilization established there, though cosmopolitan, was essentially Asian and has left its mark on all the cities of East Africa which have developed since the opening up of the interior. "Asian" in East Africa usually means either Indian or Pakistani, Moslem or Hindu, as well as the smaller Goan Catholic group [from Goa, a former Portuguese enclave in India]. Arabs are, for many purposes, also included.

The Asians have come and continue to come to East Africa because of opportunities for trade and the advantages of a better life for themselves and their children. Their contribution to the economic development of the area has been out of all proportion to their numbers.

Whereas the European has gone in to East Africa to govern, to farm, or to engage in some relatively large-scale business enterprise, the small Asian shopkeeper has penetrated right out into the villages, creating a demand for goods where none existed before, providing most of the people's needs in consumer goods and, later, sometimes branching out into larger manufacturing or farming enterprises, as in cotton ginning or the sugar plantations of Uganda.

Whereas most Europeans were more or less temporary residents, the Asians had come to stay. They may have thought of India or Pakistan as home, but this was more a sentimental than a real attachment. With the coming of independence, however, Asian immigration has decreased and emigration increased.

Two factors combine to make the Asians an object of prejudice from Africans and from Europeans. One is social and the other economic.

Many Asians are closely involved with one or other of the Asian religious sects, most of which are exclusive to themselves. They thus tend to have their own independent social and cultural life and to be cut off from many of the people among whom they live.

They are also concentrated in occupations which arouse popular envy. Characteristically they are shopkeepers and businessmen. In Tanganyika about 50 per cent of Asians are dependent on trade, in Kenya over 33 per cent, and in Uganda over 50 per cent. In both these respects they are like the Jews of Europe and are in the same danger of being subjected to discrimination. This danger needs to be closely watched both by the Asians themselves and by the new African governments. [The danger exploded into an international problem early in 1968, when the 160,000 Asians living in Kenya came under growing pressure from Kenyan authorities to leave the country. They had been offered (and many had accepted) British citizenship when Kenya gained its independence in 1963. Faced with a sudden flood of Asian immigrants, however, the British government moved to limit the number of Asians from Kenya it would actually accept. Meanwhile, Kenyan authorities seemed reluctant to ease pressure on its non-citizen Asians, who had chosen to give their loyalty to the departing colonial power rather than to the new nation in which they would reside. For additional background on this problem, see Section IV, below.—Ed.]

The Asian comes to East Africa to better himself and he usually succeeds. In doing so he also helps to improve East Africa. As the East Africa Royal Commission said:

. . . the remarkable tenacity and courage of the Indian trader has been mainly responsible for stimulating the wants of the indigenous peoples, even in the remotest areas, by opening to them a shopwindow on the modern world and for collecting for sale elsewhere whatever small surpluses are available for disposal. The non-African trading system as it exists in East Africa is one of the most important assets which the economy possesses.

THE HISTORICAL HERITAGE [3]

The logic of federation in East Africa is rooted in geographical and historical factors as well as in recent political and economic developments. Briefly, the area has an obvious geographical unity. East Africa (Tanganyika [now Tanzania], Uganda, and Kenya), comprising 642,728 square miles, is slightly smaller than the United States west of the Rocky Mountains. Tanganyika covers more than four times, and Kenya three times, the land area of Uganda. The region forms a compact block, bounded on the north by the highlands of Ethiopia, on the west by the great African lakes, and on the east by the Indian Ocean. There are no natural frontiers to mark the boundaries of each country. From historic times, trade has flowed from inland to coastal areas in a distinct East African pattern. While there are manifold diversities among the peoples, as well as significant variations in climate and topography, modern historical forces have acted to emphasize the singularity of the region despite its vastness and lack of communications.

Settlement of East Africa

Seventy-five years ago the peoples of East Africa were virtually unaware that a modern world existed outside the confining boundaries of their tribes. The civilized world was only newly acquainted with Mount Kilimanjaro and Lake Victoria through the popular books and reports of East Africa's explorers.

The opening of East Africa was the result primarily of German imperial ambitions. In the early 1880's, agents of a German-chartered colonization society concluded treaties with tribal chiefs in the interior of what is now Tanganyika. By 1885, the German government was prepared to press its claim for recognition as the predominant power in Tanganyika. Its ambitions were written into the Congo Basin Treaty of 1885 and the records of the Berlin Conference of 1884-1885.

[3] From *An East African Federation*, by Carl G. Rosberg, Jr., assistant professor of political science, University of California at Berkeley, with Aaron Segal, a former graduate student in political science at the University. (International Conciliation. no 543) Carnegie Endowment for International Peace. United Nations Plaza at 46th Street. New York 10017. '63. p 7-23. Reprinted by permission.

Before the arrival of the Germans, assertions of sovereignty over the interior of East Africa were merely nominal. The caravan routes of slave and ivory traders and the scattered huts of missionaries were the sole physical evidence of the outside world. The interior African tribes were relatively untouched by foreigners. On the coastal strip of Kenya and Tanganyika, however, there were Arab towns—some more than one thousand years old—loosely federated under the leadership of the Sultan of Zanzibar. The coastal area and the off-shore islands were the centers of a flourishing trade, based largely on ivory and slaves, with a long history of contact with Arabia, Persia, and India. The German intrusion displaced the authority of Zanzibar, which had for more than fifty years enjoyed the pro-tection of treaties with the British East India Company and the British government.

In face of this German threat, the British moved to consolidate their hold on the source of the Nile River in Uganda. The Imperial British East Africa Company was chartered, and Captain (later Lord) Lugard marched to Buganda, the center of the most advanced and thoroughly consolidated African kingdom in East Africa. Here Lugard concluded a series of treaties with the kingdoms to the north and west of Lake Victoria. With the financial collapse of the British company, these treaties reverted to the Crown and formed the basis of the Uganda protectorate which was declared in 1894. To protect its lines of communication with Uganda, the British government in 1895 created the British East Africa protectorate which comprised a large part of present-day Kenya. By 1900, both the Germans and the British had begun to lay down railways from the coast to the in-terior lakes to secure their hold over their respective spheres of in-fluence. Indian labor was recruited, particularly by the British, to build the railroads; as the lines progressed, Indian shopkeepers and traders moved into the interior of East Africa.

Land-holding Patterns

More than 6,000 European settlers were brought to German East Africa by 1909. The German research station at Amani developed the production of sisal, oil seeds, coffee, and cotton, and the plantations established by the Germans before 1914 set the pattern of exports which has persisted to the present. Little attention was given to livestock production, which was viewed as an African interest. The main thrust of German economic development was a policy of plantation development, rather than of fostering African agricultural development. The German administration was direct and authoritarian. A number of African rebellions and resistance movements were conclusively smashed, with serious consequences to African population and production that are evident today in the southern portion of Tanganyika.

The administration of Uganda contrasts sharply with that of German East Africa. Very little land was alienated to European or Asian production, and plantation organization has played a small role in Uganda. After 1900, the influences of the protectorate government, commercial interests, and the missionaries combined to encourage cotton production by African smallholders; this project was feasible in the Buganda region because of its freeholding system of tenure. Cotton production expanded unevenly, yet at a phenomenal rate, in the years before World War I. Unlike Kenya, Uganda's administration was deeply rooted in a concept of safeguarding African interests and in the theory and practice of indirect rule, complemented in certain areas with direct administration.

Kenya, or, as it was then known, the British East Africa protectorate, was a poor relative of Uganda. The railway cut through an arid, uninviting zone of scattered population, and initially Kenya was considered merely an antechamber to the Uganda protectorate. A closer view revealed the existence of fertile highlands that appeared underpopulated and ideally suited to colonization. In 1902, the extensive eastern province of Uganda, which contained a large portion of these highlands, and the populated African areas around the eastern shores of Lake Victoria were transferred to Kenya. This was apparently done to place the Uganda Railway under a single administration. But at the same time it brought nearly all the area suitable for colonization under one colonial government and thus helped to set in motion the separate historical courses of the two dependencies.

From 1903 to the outbreak of World War I and after, white settlement and alienation of land were promoted in a large block of land in high-altitude areas of southeastern Kenya. Large-scale production of sisal, sugar, coffee, maize, pyrethrum, and tea, as well as extensive grazing, were encouraged. Little attention was devoted before World War II to the potential for cash cropping by the African, whose primary role in the market economy was that of wage earner. As early as 1914, the rough outline of the land patterns that were to dominate Kenya's development could be discerned. The "white highlands" were, by administrative arrangements, available exclusively for European settlement, while African tribal leaders received guarantees that laid the groundwork for the establishment of distinct African tribal reserves. Asians, prohibited from holding land in the white highlands, became traders, artisans, and clerks in the government.

Following World War I and the ending of German rule in Tanganyika, the broad political framework of East Africa was discernible. The area was now entirely under British suzerainty, with each territory not only having a different legal status but pursuing its own distinct pattern of development. Tanganyika, which was to become a trust territory after World War II, was a mandate under British administration. While Uganda remained a protectorate in which the predominance of African influence was recognized, Kenya's status was changed to that of a crown colony in which white settler influence was entrenched and dominant. Kenya's coastal strip which extends some ten miles inland and stretches from the Tanganyika border to the Tana River has been administered as an integral part of Kenya, although it . . . [was] legally a protectorate and . . . [belonged] to the Sultan of Zanzibar, to whom Britain . . . paid £16,000 a year . . . [after] 1895.

Early Efforts Toward Federation

Although the establishment of British hegemony after World War I stimulated specific proposals and public debate on closer union, federation, or administrative amalgamation (these terms tended to be used interchangeably) of East Africa, the idea of federation is much older. It may be traced back at least to the instructions given to Sir Harry Johnston as Special Commissioner to Uganda in 1899. He was to consider the merits of some form of union or amalgamation of the East African (Kenya) and Uganda protectorates, and to locate a site for a prospective federal capital. Johnston enthusiastically recommended amalgamation and his proposals received some support. However, the completion of the railway to Lake Victoria, together with the extension of Kenya territory to the lake and the placing of the railway under Kenya's administration, temporarily undermined his administrative arguments for federation. Nonetheless, the rejection of Johnston's proposal did not end the discussion or proposals for union. The Foreign Office, which was responsible for the two protectorates until 1905, continued to maintain an interest, and the Colonial Office, to which responsibility was transferred, vaguely considered federation to be desirable.

In 1905, Kenya settlers made a strong plea for amalgamation, and, in 1909, Sir Percy Girouard, the newly appointed governor of the East Africa protectorate, was ordered to inquire into its feasibility. He strongly supported federation and believed it was possible to maintain a policy that advanced European interests and at the same time defended the interests of Africans. His proposals were not accepted by the Colonial Office.

The end of World War I and the British acquisition of the mandate for Tanganyika again brought the idea of federation to the forefront. Lord Milner, then secretary of state for the colonies and a powerful figure in the British cabinet, was believed to be sympathetic to a scheme of closer union advocated by his undersecretary, L. S. Amery. Despite Amery's enthusiasm for union, first acquired during a private trip to East Africa in 1908, Lord Milner [as Amery put it] "was inclined to let things in East Africa settle down a little before taking action."

Amery's project was stillborn, but the mandate terms for Tanganyika authorized administrative union with its neighbors as long as the measures adopted to that end were consistent with the other terms of the mandate.

While unification was not a dominant concern of policy during the early years of settlement, the establishment of certain common services yielded clear economic and administrative advantages. In 1900, for example, the East Africa and Uganda protectorates amalgamated their postal services, and British East Africa as an entity became a member of the Universal Postal Union. The need for military cooperation led to the formation of the King's African Rifles in 1902, providing defense for each protectorate in East and Central Africa with a battalion in reserve. An important step toward an East African customs union came in 1917 when Uganda and Kenya merged their customs authorities. In 1922, Tanganyika adopted the common tariff ruling of Uganda and Kenya and the next year agreed to the free interchange of local produce.

In the early 1920's, there were recurring indications that closer union was a possibility, and British interest in it was spurred on by the potential economic advantages. In 1924, the East Africa Commission visited Kenya, Northern Rhodesia, Nyasaland, Tanganyika, Uganda, and Zanzibar to consider means of accelerating economic development and achieving closer coordination of policy. The Commission strongly supported the Kenya-Uganda customs union and its extension to Tanganyika, which was achieved in 1927. Although the Commission found federation to be premature, with local opinion unprepared and communications inadequately developed, it nonetheless recommended periodic conferences of governors to foster interterritorial cooperation and coordination of matters of common interest. The first governors' conference for this purpose met in 1926.

Divergent Interests

Despite the rejection of federation by the East Africa Commission, a curious mixture of both imperial and Kenya European settler interests caused the question to be exhaustively explored and debated both in East Africa and in Great Britain between 1925 and 1932. No longer was it the scheme of a few interested parties; it became for the first time a public issue in which the differences between various proposals and their underlying assumptions came into direct conflict.

L. S. Amery, by this time secretary of state for the colonies as well as the leading proponent of federation, initiated the debate by appointing Sir Edward Grigg governor of Kenya in 1925 with instructions to prepare a plan for closer union. Amery and British commercial interests in East Africa viewed federation principally as the amalgamation of certain common services to facilitate the economic development of the region to the benefit of the Empire. They felt transport and research were the keys to progress; these might be coordinated under a high commissioner for East Africa, while the British government could retain responsibility for native policy in the different territories.

Kenya's European settlers, however, viewed federation as creating a new white dominion reaching from Kenya to the Rhodesias. Their goal was internal self-government; although a minority on the Kenya legislative council, they had already achieved considerable influence over governmental policy. Lord Delamere led a contingent of settler opinion which held that federation was inevitable and that the wisest course was to support it from the outset and obtain the greatest possible benefit for Kenya. The demand for an elected European majority in the Kenya legislative council was a *sine qua non* for any scheme for closer union or federation.

By promising Kenya's European settlers an unofficial but not wholly elected majority in the legislative council, Sir Edward Grigg was able to command their support for his proposed federal council which would direct certain common services. The governor of Tanganyika, Sir Donald Cameron, threatened to resign if this plan was adopted and his threat was backed by those in Great Britain, led by Lord Lugard and J. H. Oldham, secretary of the International Missionary Council, who viewed East African problems in a different perspective. They rejected the claims of the Kenya settlers and viewed critically the subordination of African interests in Kenya as compared with Uganda and Tanganyika. This group sought a clear statement and fulfillment of the primary responsibility of the British government for the safeguarding of African interests—a responsibility that could in no way be surrendered or diminished. Moreover, there was need for a common native policy in East Africa that would build on traditional tribal institutions and native councils rather than encourage African political representation in Western political institutions.

During the next five years . . . [numerous proposals for union were made, but] a joint select committee of the two houses of Parliament . . . found that none of the proposals advanced was even moderately acceptable to all the communities in East Africa, and it recommended that formal union was out of the question for the time being. Without closer union, however, it was considered even more incumbent upon the territories to look for means of economic coordination. The committee turned to the governors' conference in this regard.

The underlying motive for rejection of closer union by the multiracial population of East Africa was fear. Rather than experiment with federation, with its attendant possibilities for widespread economic and other rewards, the individual communities clung to the status quo. Indians in Tanganyika, guaranteed equality of treatment by the League of Nations mandate under which Britain administered the territory, were afraid that any closer ties with Kenya might bring upon them the disabilities under which Indians in Kenya lived. Africans in both Uganda and Tanganyika hesitated to throw in their lot with Kenya, which had long been referred to as a "white man's country," and all of them, including those in Kenya as well, were opposed to the imposition of another authority between the territorial administration and Great Britain. Perhaps, however, the deciding factor was the opposition of European settlers in Kenya, who refused any diminution of local sovereignty without a corresponding increase in their power to control the government of Kenya.

While, for the British government, the issue of political unification was closed with the acceptance of the report of the joint select committee in 1932, renewed interest in the issue soon developed. Some European settlers in Tanganyika and Kenya in the late thirties argued that complete union of the two territories was vital in order that Tanganyika be secured for the Empire and be protected against Nazi subversion. There was some genuine and partially justified fear in East Africa that Tanganyika might be traded away to Hitler as part of a larger bargain for "peace in our time."

Of more significance for the future was the growth in the 1930's of the annual governors' conference, with its permanent secretariat, as an effective organization in promoting a joint approach to problems and issues. In the 1920's, the East African colonial governments had already found that their meager resources for scientific research could be exploited more efficiently on a pooled basis. This principle was extended by the amalgamation of the postal and telegraph services of the three territories in 1931 and the formation of an East African air service in 1937. The organization of scientific research on an interterritorial basis was also improved. Statistics, meteorology, and locust control were administered on a regional basis, as was Makerere College in Uganda, then the only institution of higher education in East Africa.

Recent Proposals

The demands of World War II upon East Africa gave rise to new interterritorial bodies and councils to direct, regulate, and coordinate the economy and manpower of Kenya, Uganda, and Tanganyika. . . .

To foster East African economic development, the British government published, in December 1945, a white paper proposing a new interterritorial organization in East Africa. Political federation was rejected, as there were no grounds for believing that common agreement existed among Kenya, Uganda, and Tanganyika. . . . Briefly, the proposals envisaged the creation of an East African high commission consisting of the governors of Kenya, Tanganyika, and Uganda, with a permanent secretariat to administer interterritorial services.

In addition to the high commission, there would be a central legislative assembly with authority to act on a scheduled list of subjects. The unofficial members of the legislative assembly "would have no power to initiate legislation but they could introduce motions on any subject under the usual rules." In addition to twelve nominated official (civil servant) members, the legislative assembly would consist of twenty-four unofficial members: six European and six Indian members, two of each to be elected by each territorial legislative council; six members, "as many as possible" to be Africans, nominated by the high commission as trustees of African interests (two from each territory); two members nominated by the high commission to represent Arab interests; and four other members nominated by the high commission.

Criticism of the proposals revolved almost entirely around the principle of equal representation of East Africa's three major racial groups. The most determined hostility came from the Kenya European community, which regarded the principle as a threat to the ideals of white settlement and its political predominance in the affairs of the colony. The attempt by the British government to build up a legislature on the basis of equality of race was unacceptable to it. On the other hand, most African and Indian opinion in Kenya, as in Uganda and Tanganyika, was favorable to the proposals for the very same reason. To Africans, equal representation was a step forward in their struggle for self-determination, while the European politicians regarded it as a dangerous precedent for the future. In the storm of opposition that raged for months, European elected leaders also rejected any proposals for a central assembly with legislative powers. While they appreciated the need for efficient interterritorial coordination for a limited number of common services, they felt this need could be fulfilled without the superimposition of an assembly on the existing territorial legislative councils. The European interests argued that Kenya should retain freedom to pursue its own internal development policy, a policy that had differed from the trend in the neighboring two territories and that had received approval from the British government.

Equality Principle as an Obstacle

In February 1947, the revised proposals for an interterritorial organization in East Africa were published. Under the new proposals, the central legislative assembly would be composed of a speaker, seven ex officio members to be officers in the high commission, three nominated official members (one from each territory) and four appointed from the unofficial members within each territorial legislative council. These four would include one representative each from the European, Indian, and African communities, with the fourth representing all the unofficials. One Arab member would be appointed by the high commission. Thus the new proposals made provision for ten instead of twelve official and thirteen unofficial members instead of twenty-four. In addition to reducing the representative quality of the assembly, the immediate effect was to strengthen European representation.

These revised proposals provoked a second outburst of protests, this time on the part of Indians and Africans in all three territories and the Europeans in Uganda. The East African Indian National Congress condemned the new proposals, described the new white paper as "this unhappy surrender" and a victory for Europeans. Kenya's Europeans generally favored the new proposals, since their commanding position in the legislative council ensured that the fourth unofficial representative would be a European.

Despite opposition to what non-Europeans regarded as the abandonment of the principle of equal representation, the acceptance of the proposals was ensured by the official members, who were a majority in each legislative council. There was a significant difference in the new proposals, not only in respect to representation, but also in the list of subjects assigned to the high commission. While Makerere College and related educational institutions, civil aviation, and meteorological services were added to the high commission central assembly list as interterritorial concerns, several important areas assigned to it in the 1945 proposals were dropped. Among these were mining, broadcasting, commercial law, industrial licensing, and agricultural marketing boards. Thus its scope of authority in influencing economic development on an East African basis was considerably reduced from what was originally envisaged.

High Commission to EACSO

The high commission came into being on 1 January 1948. While its achievements were not inconsiderable, it was never able to gain the full confidence of Africans or enlist widespread public support. In part this was due to the controversy that surrounded its origin and to its adoption over the opposition of Africans who still feared it might be employed to strengthen European influence.

The foremost achievements of the East Africa high commission were in the self-contained services (transport and communications) which provided their own revenues. The successful merger of the Kenya and Uganda railways and the Tanganyika rail line in 1948 resulted in improved service and an impressive record of overseas borrowing. The non-self-contained services (customs and excise, research and science, statistics, and others) were supported by the British government and by annual grants from the territorial colonial governments. While the increased sums appropriated by the latter represented expressions of confidence, specific services were often subject to sharp criticism in territorial legislative councils. The need to obtain prior approval of all three colonial governments also limited the central assembly's ability to pass interterritorial legislation.

The growth and spread of African nationalism and its ability to affect the direction and pace of political development in the East African territories created a new situation by the late 1950's. The future of a colonial interterritorial organization, commanding little support from African nationalists, seemed very questionable with the prospect of each territory becoming a separate independent state. Indeed, some of its services and benefits had even begun to be questioned. The idea of an eventual federation of East Africa was recognized at the first meeting of the Pan-African Freedom Movement of East and Central Africa (PAFMECA) in 1958, but the struggle for African self-determination was then the dominant issue and focus of attention. Julius Nyerere, President of the Tanganyika African National Union (TANU), recognizing the dangers to pan-Africanism of breaking established interterritorial links and institutions, was the first to advocate a possible relationship of the high commission to a future East African federation. While many African leaders were still hesitant about the high commission, Nyerere specifically endorsed it in 1959 as the foundation for a future federation. Only by federation could the real benefits conveyed by the high commission be preserved and redistributed more equitably within a politically new East Africa.

Nyerere saw as an immediate danger to the goal of federation the uneven pace of political development in each territory. As this danger became more evident in 1960, he argued for accelerated political advancement in Uganda and Kenya, and even offered to delay the independence of Tanganyika to enable the other two territories to catch up so that all three could achieve independence and federation at the same time. He expressed the fear that were they to gain independence at different times, the effect might be to arouse national sentiments which would make negotiation of a federation far more difficult. Moreover, he considered that an independent sovereign state could not accept the degree of loss of control over its own policies implicit in continued association with two colonial countries in the high commission.

Although the internal political difficulties of Kenya and Uganda inhibited the acceleration of a transfer of power, an economic and constitutional framework was devised in 1961 which permitted Tanganyika to obtain independence and at the same time maintain the interterritorial structure as a basis for a future federation. During 1960, a searching investigation was made into interterritorial economic cooperation by the East African Economic and Fiscal Commission (the Raisman commission). The gist of its proposals was to preserve and strengthen this cooperation while providing the broadest possible scope for development of the national economies by the emerging new states. The findings and recommendations of this commission provided the basis for the constitution of the East African Common Services Organization (EACSO) which was accepted by the East African delegations at the London Conference in June 1961.

Africans Take Up Theme

The change from the high commission to EACSO was a change from a colonial institution to a political organization built upon the representative institutions of the East African countries. Where the high commission was controlled by the colonial governors, EACSO consists of a triumvirate—an executive council of ministers composed of three principal ministers from Tanganyika, Uganda, and Kenya—supported by separate ministerial triumvirates for communications and transport, finance, commerce and industry, and social services. To obtain the greatest possible public support for the organization, the central legislative assembly is composed of twenty-seven elected members (nine members from each territory elected by the territorial legislatures) as well as the twelve ministers who are members of the four triumvirates. The assembly has powers to legislate over the common services and responsibilities of the organization.

THE LOGIC OF FEDERATION [4]

East Africa's contact with the outside world dates back some two millennia. Arab slave traders and hunters were active in this part of Africa from about the first century A.D., although actual colonization of the coast did not begin until six or seven centuries later. The Portuguese wrested power from Arab rulers during the 1500's, only to relinquish it a hundred years later. Until the partition of the area among European nations toward the end of the last century, the East African coast was ruled by the Sultan of Zanzibar, with the interior controlled by numerous tribal chiefs. During the late 1800's, British and German explorers and merchants gradually carved out national spheres of interest through concessions arranged with Arab rulers and local tribes; these arrangements were formalized by an agreement between the British and German governments in 1890, which gave the region later to be known as Tanganyika to Germany, with Britain retaining control of what is now Kenya, Uganda, and Zanzibar.

Early efforts to settle and develop these areas were made by two private organizations, the British East Africa Company and the German East Africa Company; colonial rule followed in the 1890's. After World War I, Tanganyika was transferred from German to British rule under a mandate from the League of Nations, and later from the United Nations. The four states gained increasing degrees of self-government, culminating in complete independence

[4] From *East and Central Africa—A Survey of Six Developing Countries.* Foreign Information Service. First National City Bank. New York. '66. p 2-6. Reprinted by permission.

within the Commonwealth in the early 1960's—Tanganyika in 1961, Uganda in 1962, and Zanzibar and Kenya in 1963. Two of these states united early in 1964 to form the United Republic of Tanganyika and Zanzibar, or Tanzania.

Farther south, a similar pattern of exploration and private development followed by colonial rule occurred in the Rhodesias. European settlement began in 1890 with the arrival from the south of a pioneer column sponsored by the British South Africa Company, organized by Cecil Rhodes and acting under a royal charter. The Company administered the two Rhodesias until 1923, when Southern Rhodesia became a self-governing colony and Northern Rhodesia a British protectorate. Nyasaland had come under British influence in the latter half of the 1800's, and became a protectorate in the opening years of this century, following the signing of treaties between the British government and local chiefs.

In 1953, the three states joined in the almost entirely self-governing Federation of Rhodesia and Nyasaland, which existed until the end of 1963. Northern Rhodesia and Nyasaland gained full independence from Britain during 1964, adopting respectively the names of Zambia and Malawi. Southern Rhodesia, denied this status because of insufficient progress toward effective African participation in government, unilaterally declared its independence in November 1965. At this writing, Britain is leading an international effort—involving drastic economic sanctions—to restore the former political framework in Rhodesia.

Moves Toward Regional Cooperation

The English-speaking states of East Africa have a long tradition of cooperation in economic matters. During the years of British colonial administration, many vital economic functions were performed jointly for Kenya, Uganda, and Tanganyika. Trade flowed freely within the area, and the currency in use in all three countries was issued by a centralized institution. Against this background of economic integration, discussions concerning a political federation of the three states were a logical development after independence had been achieved. Although plans for a federal government are currently dormant, political unity in East Africa remains a long-range goal.

Free trade between Kenya and Uganda was inaugurated in 1917, and a combined customs authority formed. Over the years, Tanganyika gradually became a partner to these arrangements. During the same period, the need to coordinate economic development, research, and transport and communications gained recognition, and the scope of cooperation widened. These joint activities were formalized in 1948 under the East Africa High Commission, which became the East African Common Services Organization (EACSO), headquartered in Nairobi, in 1961 after Tanganyika achieved full independence.

This body is headed by an authority made up of the president of Tanzania and the prime ministers of Kenya and Uganda. Five committees oversee groups of services performed jointly for the three member states:

1. Communications, including railways, shipping and harbors, air transport, mail services, and telecommunications
2. Finance, mainly the collection of customs duties and excise and income taxes
3. Commercial and industrial coordination
4. Research services
5. Labor, including industrial relations

Transport and communications are considered "self-contained services" financed through charges levied on users; the rest are supported by funds provided by the East African and British governments. For the fiscal year ended last March [1965], the British financial contribution to the EACSO amounted to slightly over $17 million. A central legislative assembly is responsible for legislation required to carry out the common services.

Desire for Unity

The heads of all three countries have stated their desire to maintain these services on an integrated basis. However, cooperation in some other important sectors has suffered . . . [during 1964-65]. At independence, a functioning common market existed among

Kenya, Uganda, and Tanganyika. Intra-area trade was free of customs duties. Although no formal common external tariff had been drawn up, in practice tariff schedules of the three members had been approximately aligned through joint negotiations. A common monetary system was also in effect for these three countries and for Zanzibar. The common currency in use—the East African shilling, officially at par with sterling, but divided into one hundred cents—was issued by the East African Currency Board in Nairobi. The Board also held the international reserves of the area, primarily in the form of sterling balances in London.

Today, the common currency system is being dismantled, while the East African Common Market is undergoing severe stresses. [For a more recent (and optimistic) view, see the next article in this compilation.—Ed.] Tanzania last year announced that it would withdraw from the East African Currency Board and introduce its own monetary system. This action forced Kenya and Uganda to follow suit, and separate central banks should be functioning in each of the three countries by mid-1966. Foreign exchange reserves held by the Board will be apportioned among the new central banks. Last June [1965] the three countries extended to all other sterling area members the same exchange control regulations formerly applied only to nonsterling countries. At the same time, Tanzania imposed restrictions on a wide variety of imports from Kenya and Uganda. In part, this move was aimed at ending the country's chronic imbalance in intra-area trade. It was also meant to stimulate domestic industry, and to clear the way for increased imports from mainland China under the terms of an aid agreement with that country.

This weakening of the important economic ties between the states stems from the failure to reach agreement after independence on the formation of a political East African Federation, partly due to fears of domination by Kenya, the most economically advanced member of the group. Tanzania had firmly supported a strong federal government for the three states in the hope that the central government would provide development assistance which would enable the country to catch up industrially with Kenya, and thereby shrink its considerable trade deficit with its two partners—a deficit that dissipated the foreign exchange accruing from an export surplus with the rest of the world. Despite a compromise pact to locate the bulk of new industry in Uganda and Tanganyika, basic differences concerning the nature and degree of authority of a central government make it appear unlikely that any progress toward the Federation will be made in the foreseeable future.

Prospect of New Arrangements

The restrictions on trade among the three countries, coupled with the breakup of their common monetary system, have dealt the East African Common Market a hard blow. Nevertheless, there is hope that new and viable arrangements can be made. The leaders of Kenya, Uganda, and Tanzania, who have repeatedly called for continued regional cooperation, recently appointed a former Danish minister of economics as the independent chairman of a special commission on East African cooperation charged with examining the working of the common services and common market. . . .

The breakup of the Federation of Rhodesia and Nyasaland virtually abolished the economic and monetary integration of this area. Following the dissolution of the Federation, all of the administrative functions formerly performed by the federal government in Salisbury reverted to the individual Central African states, with the exception of Central African Airways, Rhodesia Railways, Central African Power Corporation (successor to the Federal Power Board), and the Agricultural Research Council. The Bank of Rhodesia and Nyasaland, which had issued the common currency circulating in the Federation, was dissolved and its assets divided among three national central banks. These now issue separate currencies—Zambian, Malawi, and Rhodesian pounds, at par with sterling—and the Federation currency is no longer legal tender.

Following Rhodesia's unilateral declaration of independence (UDI), the country was expelled from the sterling area and suspended from the Commonwealth preferential trading arrangements. Zambia has joined in the economic sanctions currently being imposed on Rhodesia. Regardless of the outcome of UDI, the political strains of the past months will undoubtedly hinder future efforts to restore normal relations between Rhodesia and her former partners.

Hopes for a Wider Cooperation

Despite these setbacks, the desire for closer economic cooperation in East and Central Africa remains strong, based both on a history of working together, and the need to overcome handicaps imposed by the small size of individual national markets. Late ... [in 1965], representatives of Kenya, Malawi, Tanzania, Uganda, and Zambia met with delegates from Burundi, Ethiopia, Rwanda, and Mauritius at Lusaka, Zambia, in a conference sponsored by the UN Economic Commission for Africa to explore possibilities for mutual cooperation within an area broadly defined as East Africa. Agreement was reached to work towards the establishment of an East African Economic Community, and to designate a council of ministers to draw up a treaty defining the nature and scope of the organization. The treaty is expected to establish the framework for coordination of activities in industry, agriculture, transport and communications, trade and payments, use of manpower, and development of natural resources. A key feature of the proposed Community is the progressive elimination within a ten-year period of internal trade barriers and the negotiation of a common external tariff.

With the exception of Rhodesia, the countries . . . [of East Africa] are also members of the wider, but more politically oriented, Organization of African Unity (OAU). Thus they participate in three tiers of cooperative arrangements: the East African common services and common market, or the remaining economic links among the former Federation states; the proposed East African Economic Community; and the virtually Africa-wide grouping of independent states within the OAU. Undoubtedly, the passage of time will eventually sort out these relationships and clarify the dominant future patterns of economic and political cooperation in East and Central Africa. . . .

AN EAST AFRICAN COMMON MARKET [5]

Kenya, Uganda and Tanzania formally inaugurated the East African Community today [December 1, 1967] in a cautious move back to the common market these three countries enjoyed when all were part of the British Empire.

Zambia has formally asked the three countries for some form of association with the new Community. [See "Zambia Draws Closer to East Africa," in Section V, below.] Presidents Jomo Kenyatta of Kenya, Milton Obote of Uganda and Julius K. Nyerere of Tanzania each received similar letters from Kenneth D. Kaunda, the Zambian leader.

For Zambia, there is a special incentive to try to break loose from her dependence on Rhodesia, South Africa and Portugal's African possessions for supplies and for transport of her copper to the sea. In Zambia, as in the rest of black Africa, there is a growing determination to halt political and economic fragmentation.

Under the sponsorship of the United Nations Economic Commission for Africa, vague terms of association in the Economic Community of Eastern Africa have already been ratified by ten countries in the region.

In Central Africa, Cameroon, the Central African Republic, Chad, Gabon and the former Belgian Congo, have had a customs union and common external tariff and development policies since the beginning of last year [1966], and now have a common central bank. . . .

And in West Africa, twelve countries have signed an agreement to coordinate their economic development.

But none of these groups has the advantages of the community that was inaugurated this morning in Arusha, an unpretentious town on the lower slopes of Mount Meru in northern Tanzania, which is to be the headquarters of the new group.

[5] From "3 East African Nations Inaugurate Trade Bloc," by Lawrence Fellows, staff correspondent. New York *Times.* p 8. D. 2, '67. © 1967 by The New York Times Company. Reprinted by permission.

Market of 27 Million People

This is the second attempt these countries have made to halt the forces of political and economic disintegration. Even with the great stress on "nation building," on internal economic and political development and on the need for national consciousness, political leaders and the business community were aware of the need to hang together.

To attract new industries and to give their own infant industries a chance, they would find it more advantageous to offer a single potential market of 27 million people instead of separate markets of 8 million in Uganda, 9 million in Kenya and 10 million in Tanzania.

The trouble was that Kenya always got the lion's share in every cooperative economic venture; Nairobi, capital of Kenya and in many ways of East Africa, has what investors seem to need: transportation and communications facilities, space, water, lots of available labor and very pleasant living conditions.

Because Kenya needs as much of this wider East African market as she can hang on to, she agreed in Kampala, the Uganda capital, in 1964 that the three countries should decide together where new industries should be situated.

Unfortunately, new investors would not be told where to go. The idea fell apart so quickly that the agreement was never ratified. Tanzania and then Uganda threw up walls of tariffs and quotas to block out goods from Kenya. Eventually the three broke up their common currency and set up independent monetary authorities.

II. THE POLITICS OF INDEPENDENCE

EDITOR'S INTRODUCTION

Others have observed that politics in Africa today is largely a matter of personalities, rather than parties, institutions, or factions. Nkrumah in Ghana, Sekou Touré in Guinea, Haile Selassie in Ethiopia, Senghor in Senegal—men rather than movements seem to rule this continent, just as personalities rather than parties seem to characterize the various countries.

Such is the case in East Africa, where Jomo Kenyatta in Kenya, Julius Nyerere in Tanzania, and A. Milton Obote in Uganda have come to personify, in their own images, the political systems of the nations they rule. Each of these men is great in his own right. Kenyatta, nearing eighty, once the dread symbol of the Mau Mau, is today the jovial, friendly leader of East Africa's most stable, prosperous, and pro-Western state. Nyerere, an intellectual, beloved of his own people and fully aware of the snares of absolute power, is struggling to instill in his own nation the spirit of dedication and sacrifice that animates his own behavior. Obote, brilliant if unstable, evinces classic characteristics associated with the humble risen to the seat of power—he is distrustful, ruthless, and wholly dedicated to the welfare of those he claims to represent. As a study in character analysis, East African politics could not be more fascinating to the Western observer.

This section probes the post-independence politics of Kenya, Tanzania, and Uganda as reflected in the personalities of (and the problems facing) their leaders. In the first article a New York *Times* correspondent draws a likable portrait of Kenya's Jomo Kenyatta, the quintessence of whose political program is summarized in the Swahili word *Harambee*—"let's all pull together." Next, an *Atlantic* Report on Tanzania explains the motives and methods of Julius Nyerere and the political system his personality is imprinting upon Tanzania. In the final article, a journalist and novelist

delves into the character and background of Uganda's remarkable
leader, A. Milton Obote, and the nature of the state he is forging
for his people.

KENYA UNDER JOMO KENYATTA [1]

When Jomo Kenyatta was a boy in Ichaweri, he used to herd
cattle on the pasture around Mogumo-wa-njathi, the only sacred
tree left in his neighborhood. There were other trees around, but
no sacred ones, for the British settlers, in clearing their newly acquired plots for cultivation, had cut down all the sacred ones except
Mogumo-wa-njathi. It was the only tree left around Ichaweri
where the Kikuyu could make sacrifices for rain, or where com-
munion of any sort could be had with Ngai, the Divider of the
Universe.

People would come to the tree and lament: *"Gikuyu harea
keari kianoimaho."* (The Kikuyu are no longer where they used to
be.) The restless hot-tempered little cowherd would sometimes run
from the pasture in anger and shame for his tribe, and wonder how
long Ngai, sitting up there on his resting place atop Mount Kenya,
would put up with the intruding whites.

The land was eventually to be handed back, but not until after
Jomo Kenyatta had developed a fearsome, somewhat overstated
reputation as the "evil-eyed leader of Mau Mau," a "wenching,
hard-drinking, blood-letting terrorist" bent on "plunging Kenya
back into the abyss of primitive and debased tribalism." Sir Patrick
Renison, a British governor of Kenya in Mau Mau days, accused
Jomo Kenyatta of leading his people into "darkness and death."

Yet, as though some splendid Kikuyu magician had filled his
horn with the secret ingredients of the love potion they call *mon-
yenye* and spread it around the world—at least around the Western
part of the world—Kenyatta, now president of independent Kenya,
has become the image of stability and sweet reasonableness in a
continent sorely in need of just those virtues.

[1] From " 'Harambee,' Says Kenyatta—'Let's All Pull Together,' " by Lawrence Fellows, staff correspondent. New York *Times Magazine*. p 36-7+. N. 7, '65. Copyright
© 1965 by The New York Times Company. Reprinted by permission.

And Kenya, as much as any place in black Africa, holds out the prospect of a stable, more prosperous future. On vast dun-colored plains and in hot valleys scoured deep in the earth's crust, primitive tribesmen still herd their tiny humpbacked cattle as they have for centuries, but more and more of their children are being lured into school. On red, eroded hillsides, smoke rises through the thatch of clustered mud-and-wattle huts, but roads now wind up to some of them. And some of the farmers are beginning to plant not just enough corn and beans to keep alive but crops to sell as well.

In Nairobi, tall hotels and modern office buildings have sprouted from an underbrush of close-packed Indian shops and tin-roofed shacks, and African policemen direct the choking traffic with cool efficiency. Gradually, Africans are taking over jobs in the banks, the shops, customs, the post office and elsewhere. But Kenyatta is holding back the impatient tide of envious Africans wanting the jobs that white men still hold, and is thereby keeping a modicum of efficiency that other newly independent African countries might well envy.

In the cool, rolling hills of the highlands, Africans have been settled on more than one thousand farms that used to belong to white men. The farms were bought by the Kenya government, with the help of loans and grants from the British government, and in most cases broken into smaller units and resold to Africans with generous loans to get them started. On some of these farms, what used to be lawns and flower gardens are now planted with corn; what used to be smooth meadows or rich fields of grain are now reverting tragically to bush. But more often the farms are being run as well by the Africans as they ever were before.

Perhaps five hundred white farmers have found buyers on the open market, but close to one thousand remain, many of them beset by problems of thieving and drunken vandalism and by squatters inching in on the edges of the fields. There is no official pressure on the farmers to leave. Indeed, Kenyatta wants the process to be gradual, so that the inevitable temporary dislocations in food supply will not cause his people to go hungry, or seriously crimp Kenya's earnings from agricultural exports. Lesser politicians than Kenyatta are telling the squatters that the land is theirs by right, but the president is firm in his insistence that none of the farms will be had unless they are paid for.

Socialism—Kenya-Style

In a basic policy statement on Kenya's brand of African social-ism, Kenyatta has moralized on how public ownership is as prone to abuses as is private ownership. He has also said that national-ization does not always lead to additional resources, and that there will be no nationalization in Kenya without full compensation.

He has faced up to the political extremists in his country, and taken steps to cut off their supplies of Chinese and Russian money. He has suppressed the Lumumba Institute, a political training center established . . . [in 1965] mainly through the efforts of Vice President . . . [Ajuma Oginga Odinga] with help from the Soviet Union. It had a faculty of two Russians and eight Moscow-trained Africans, and a student body drawn from branches of the Kenya African National Union, the country's only political party; Ken-yatta reckoned it would be only a matter of time before the party machinery was in the hands of Communists and their sympathizers.

When a team of Russian military advisers wanted to stay in Kenya longer than Kenyatta deemed appropriate, he sent them packing. When Chou En-lai resurrected his famous remark about how Africa was ripe for revolution, Kenyatta replied sharply: "Kenya intends to avert all revolutions irrespective of their origins."

He has taken his campaign against communism—and against all he thinks threatens to undermine the country—through the ranks of the politicians, to the elders of all the tribes, and to the people. Not long ago, before tens of thousands of his countrymen who had gathered in Nairobi to hear him, Kenyatta declared that there was no place for communism in Kenya, that communism represented no less a threat to the freedom of Africans than did imperialism in its heyday.

It is naïve to think that there is no danger of imperialism from the East . . . [he said]. This is why we reject communism. It is in fact the reason why we have chosen for ourselves the policy of nonalignment and African socialism.

It is a sad mistake to think that you can get more food, more hospitals or schools by crying "communism." ...

On the platform, shifting the weight of his elephantine frame from one foot to the other, waving his fly whisk lazily to emphasize a point, he seemed huge, relaxed, powerful. This was Mzee—the Old Man—as the people call him with all the respect that accrues to age in this part of the world. (Kenyatta himself is not sure of his age; he thinks that "about seventy-five" is close.) His bleary, slow-moving eyes went back and forth over the audience, and the crowd hung on every word.

His target was those who have been building a following for themselves by preaching that all the things the people want will be theirs if they just hold out for communism. "There is no room here for the lazy or idle," Kenyatta said. "There is no room for those who wait for things to be given for nothing. There is no place for leaders who hope to build a nation on slogans."

He also was after those in Kenya who seek to follow more closely the examples set by Tanzania and Uganda. To Kenyatta's way of thinking, the union of Tanganyika with Zanzibar, and Tanzania's commitment to the various liberation movements she harbors reflect a preoccupation with the old perils of imperialism and opened new lines of Chinese penetration—just as Uganda's dispute with the Congo led to the shipment of Chinese weapons into Uganda. While Tanzania and Uganda made overtures to the East, Kenyatta did his best to tighten Kenya's connections with the West. He does not see nonalignment achieved best by breaking all the old bonds.

I must warn those in our country who seek to create confusion [he said]. It is true that we have passed through many years of Western imperialism. It is natural that we should detest Western colonialism, and associate the word *imperialism* with the West. But if we are truly nonaligned we must not avoid making friends with those Western countries which extend an honest field of cooperation and trade. To do this is just to prove that we are not free and cannot separate good from bad. It proves that we still suffer from a colonial mentality.

Kenyatta's Background

Kenyatta had been up that morning since six o'clock, pulling weeds out of a field of corn by his new house in Ichaweri. As usual, one of his aides had to get up early, too, and talk to the president about his program for that day. "I know about communism," Kenyatta said. "I've seen it, and cannot be fooled." By 8:15 his aides and his five bodyguards were ready to start the thirty-mile trip they make every morning down to Nairobi, and Kenyatta was still on the subject of communism. "I know how it works," he insisted.

He had been exposed to it only marginally at first, soon after he landed a job in Nairobi in 1921, as an inspector of water supplies. He was burning with ambition to do something about emancipating his people. He began promoting the idea of independent schools for the Kikuyu (he himself had attended a Church of Scotland mission school), and was brushed almost immediately into the turmoil of politics.

By 1928, Kenyatta was general secretary of the Kikuyu Central Association, and emerging as the real leader of the first nationalist movement in Kenya.

A group of Indians with Communist connections put up the money and legal help Kenyatta needed to go off to London and plead the Kikuyu case with Britain's colonial secretary. The Indians, with a larger community in Kenya than the British, calculated that if Kenyatta could wangle some advantages for his people, they were bound to benefit as well.

Kenyatta never got to see the colonial secretary, but fell in with the League Against Imperialism, a Communist group with headquarters in London. He paid a quick trip to Moscow, was given a handful of introductions to Communists whom he looked up in Berlin, and went to Hamburg to play a minor role at the Communist-sponsored International Negro Workers' Congress. After eighteen months, Kenyatta's Indian backers tired of supporting him. He returned to Kenya in 1930, but only to bounce back to London again the following year.

This time he stayed away from his homeland for fifteen years, presenting petitions to the Colonial Office, writing letters to the newspapers, ventilating African grievances in Trafalgar Square to anyone who would listen. In 1933 he spent four months in the Soviet Union absorbing a little more about the tactics of revolution, meeting new friends.

For a while, in London, he shared a flat near Charing Cross with Paul Robeson, the American singer and actor, and even appeared with him in a film. . . . Kenyatta played the part of a native chief, and before long he discovered that his African robes were good not only for film work, but for invitations to cocktail parties. It seemed just the thing for a man who had to scratch around both for jobs and for people to hear out his grievances against colonial rule.

Kenyatta lectured on the Workers' Educational Association circuit, and landed a job on the faculty of a Quaker college in Birmingham. Although he never got an undergraduate degree, he completed a graduate course in anthropology at the London School of Economics, and wrote a book, *Facing Mount Kenya,* a pioneering study of the customs of his people.

When the war broke out, Kenyatta took a job as a farm laborer in Sussex, and was promptly given the nickname "Jumbo" because of his bulk. He is remembered there as a good-natured chap, given to reciting verses from Rudyard Kipling—of all people—and to reading from Shakespeare's *Othello.*

Kenyatta had left two wives behind in Kenya, where polygamy is an accepted practice, and he took another while he was working in Sussex. She was Edna Grace Clark, whom he had met when they were on the same lecture circuit, and who was working then at a school in the neighborhood. She bore Kenyatta a son, but both wife and child stayed behind when Kenyatta returned to his homeland in 1946 to get back into the swim of politics. He took a fourth wife, Ngina, soon after his return.

His devotion to Ngina is almost legend. He hurries out of his office each day by four P.M., unless there is a real crisis to keep him longer, and he does not take his work home with him. He has no really close friends outside his family, and spends all his affection on Ngina and their four children, though he has not forsaken his other wives and keeps in close touch with them and with his other children.

Prison and Independence

During his long absence in England Kenyatta had become established as a symbol of African nationalism. Tens of thousands of Kikuyu came to know the name of the man who was the champion of their cause, and gave what money they could to keep the struggle alive. Now, upon his return, he led the demand for elected African representation in the legislative council. He wanted African voters on the electoral rolls. He wanted all manifestations of color discrimination abolished, and he wanted Africans back in the highland preserves of the white farmers.

But the colonial government was making no concessions, and while Kenyatta was talking of constitutional change, many of his followers were taking gruesome oaths to kill the white man, or terrify him into leaving the country. Inevitably, Kenyatta was singled out by the government as the mastermind of Mau Mau, the terrorist movement that engulfed Kenya in the early 1950's. In the predawn hours of October 20, 1952, the police, thinking to surprise him in his sleep, found him fully dressed and waiting stoically to be arrested. They bundled him off by airplane to Lokitaung, a tiny, desert post in the contorted, lifeless landscape of Kenya's north.

To hear him tell of his seven years of imprisonment at Lokitaung, they must have been the most harrowing of his life. When their frustrations piled up, he and his fellow prisoners brawled until the sun burned the energy from them. Then they would sink into apathy. Kenyatta lived in fear that he would be poisoned by the British. At night he would lie in terror, watching for scorpions or snakes, finally drifting off to sleep, as he puts it now, "hoping for the best." The worst terror, as he often recalls, was having to dig what he was told was to be his own grave.

When his sentence was completed, he was moved to Lodwar, still in the remote north, and given a little cottage and even an allowance with which to buy approved newspapers and books. From Lodwar he was eventually flown to Maralal, a mountain oasis closer to Nairobi, and then to . . . his home district.

On August 15, 1961, when he was finally released, he was a personality towering above all others. A whole generation had grown to manhood without ever seeing Jomo Kenyatta, but they accepted him as the leader of the country, the symbol of an emerging nation. His home at Ichaweri had been razed, and turned by the British into an experimental farm, but it remained a shrine the whole time. Thousands of Kikuyu cheered his return, and brought him gifts of goats, pigs, sheep, cows and baskets of corn. The British speeded the transfer of power to the Africans and on Independence Day, December 11, 1963, the man who had gone to jail before the Mau Mau committed their first white murder was able to say to a mass of cheering people: "I have snatched you out of the lion's belly."

A One-Party State

Since then, he has striven to keep his people from falling into anyone else's clutches. He has created a one-party state to transcend tribalism, to build a national unity that would offer security and opportunity to Africans of whatever tribe, to Indians, Arabs, even to Englishmen who are prepared to identify themselves with Kenya. He wants a nation impervious to the divisions which foreigners from East or West might be tempted to exploit.

He has taken on a monumental task, for the mass of Africans in Kenya have little in common beyond poverty, ignorance and disease—the three things Kenyatta describes as the greatest enemies of the country.

There are probably close to nine million Africans in Kenya of diverse origin, tradition, even language. There are Bantu, like the Kikuyu, who wandered into Kenya from West and Central Africa centuries ago. But the Bantu vary from the tall, proud Baluhya near Lake Victoria to the short, introverted Nyika of the coast. The Nilotic tribesmen who came up the Nile Valley from the Sudan are spread through Kenya from Uganda to Tanzania. Hamitic tribes like the Somali have penetrated deep into the country from the rugged northern desert. The Wanderobo, unrelated to any of the others, are the hapless indigenous remnant of Kenya's forest hunters.

In all the years the British were here, their language never penetrated deeper than the houseboys and a thin veneer of official-dom. Swahili, a Bantu-based language laced with Arabic, English and half a dozen other tongues, comes closer to being a generally used language. Not everyone speaks Swahili, but in nearly every village there is someone who understands it.

Kenyatta is using these two languages to forge unity of a sort in his country. Now even a Kikuyu boy who lapses into his own language in a classroom is likely to get his knuckles rapped by a Kikuyu teacher.

As proud as Kenyatta is of his own tribal heritage, he feels that eventually it will have to be trampled on if the old tribal argu-ments are to be forgotten, and if feelings of insecurity are not going to be aroused among the country's 49,000 Europeans, or among the 183,000 Asians whose forebears came from the Indian subcontinent at the beginning of the century to help build the railway, or among the 36,000 Arabs whose ancestors had been traders and merchants along the coast for centuries. . . .

Where there has been racial hatred, it must be ended [Kenyatta said in a broadcast before independence]. Where there has been tribal animos-ity, it will be finished. Let us not dwell upon the bitterness of the past. I would rather look to the future, to the good new Kenya, not to the bad old days. If we can create this sense of national direction and identity, we shall have gone a long way toward solving our economic problems. We hold out no empty promises of achieving utopia overnight. What we hold out to every citizen is the prospect of work, justly rewarded.

Domestic Program

The call for hard work is a main brace in Kenyatta's domestic program. It is his answer to the whisperings of other politicians that there are still some splendid properties that could be had from the Europeans and Asians for the taking. Hard work, according to the president, is the way to keep the people out of the clutches of the young radicals. It is the way to political stability, which is prerequisite to attracting foreign investment. It is necessary medi-cine in a country still too full of subsistence farmers, too close in memory to the time when outsiders initiated all progress.

On his weekend tours of the country, Kenyatta makes a point of visiting village "self-help" projects for schools, clinics, roads and the like, renewing the demand for greater effort, lecturing pointedly to the crowds on the particular sins of the neighborhood, whether drinking, cattle thieving, fighting between tribes or whatever. They come from miles around for a glimpse of Mzee, and to be caught up in his spellbinding oratory. "Harambee!" he always shouts at the end of his talks. This is Kenyatta's slogan, drawn from the loggers' Swahili word for "Let's all pull together." "Harambee!" the crowd invariably shouts back.

His position at home is unassailable, in spite of some setbacks. He had to call in the British . . . [in 1964] to help him suppress a rebellious army, an act that hurt his standing in the rest of Africa. The American-Belgian rescue mission at Stanleyville . . . [in 1964] was carried out when Kenyatta thought he still had a chance to persuade the Congolese rebels to release their hostages, and that hurt his pride. His dream of an East African political federation has slipped into oblivion.

Kenyatta's idea of nonalignment is not, as it is elsewhere in Africa, to court the East, either to make up for the old injustices of the West, or to balance a preponderance of Western influence. His idea is to keep his nose out of sensitive points in the cold war where they do not affect Kenya. Thus, he would not be likely to make quick, unsolicited pronouncements on the American involvement in Vietnam or the Dominican Republic.

Yet he does demand stronger measures from the British against Rhodesia. He offers his support to the "freedom fighters" picking at Mozambique. He may be disillusioned with the Congolese rebels, but he is still unreconciled to the use of white mercenaries by the Congolese government, or to the help the American government gives it. Still, taking all his problems into consideration, Jomo Kenyatta would seem to be as good a man to be holding the reins of power in Kenya as any Westerner could hope to see.

Some of the Western admirers would like to see him step more firmly on what would appear to be the almost contemptuously insubordinate activities of Vice President Odinga. But their differences are more tribal and personal than ideological, in spite of the friendship Odinga professes for the Russians and Chinese, in spite of his statement that communism is "food" to him. The vice president is first and foremost a Luo, the leader of Kenya's second biggest tribe. If Kenyatta were to step on him, he would risk bringing to life the ogre of tribalism he is working so hard to destroy. Instead, he has worked assiduously to isolate Odinga and to pull the rug from under his supporters in other tribes.

Dealing With Parliament

Kenyatta has not had to worry much about parliament, which is elected only once in five years, and where support for him is overwhelming. Only once did Odinga make some inroads into Kenyatta's majority, when the president was asking for support for an East African federation. As soon as Kenyatta saw the danger signs he began an enormous personal effort to win over the backbenchers, and did so with amazing success.

Odinga can now hardly work up the nerve to attend cabinet meetings, where the president leans heavily toward the ministers most suspicious of communism, and shows most demonstratively his desire to rise above tribalism. Tom Mboya, his minister for economic development, is a Luo. James Gichuru, the finance minister, is a Kikuyu, as are Dr. Gikonyo Kiano, the minister for commerce, and Attorney General Charles Njonjo. Lawrence Sagini, the minister for local government, is a Kisii. Dr. Njoroge Mungal, the defense minister, is a Kikuyu. Daniel Arap Moi, the home affairs minister, is a Kipsigis.

Among them they have built what would appear to be an interest in the West in investing in Kenya, and an interest in Kenya in looking to the West for security. Since the army mutiny, Kenyatta has built up a paramilitary police force far more formidable than the army, and he feels surer of the loyalty of the police. The United States is equipping this force with its own air transport so that it will be independently mobile.

Curiously, even the reasons Kenyatta gave last year for wanting a one-party state had a ring of friendliness to the West.

We reject a blueprint of the Western model of a two-party system of government [he said] because we do not subscribe to the notion of the government and the governed being in opposition to one another, one clamoring for duties and the other crying for rights.

Nor are we prepared to justify our predilection for a one-party system of government by using the fragile argument that parties are the expression of social classes and that therefore there must be only one party. The theory of class struggle has no relevance to our particular situation here. In a one-party state such as we envisage, we hold that politics is a potent instrument: it is through our political institutions that we influence economic trends, and not the other way around.

"Don't be fooled," a member of his Cabinet said a while ago. "Mzee was an African nationalist in the days of Mau Mau and he still is. He does not stand in East or West, even if it seems that way. He stands in Africa with both feet, and he cares for the people of Africa as he does for his own children."

TANZANIA UNDER JULIUS NYERERE [2]

The East African country of Tanzania began early . . . [in 1967] to do what few countries ever do: put its principles into practice. Theoretically Socialist since independence was granted in 1962, but displaying for the last several years a tendency to yearn for the ways of capitalism, it is now undergoing a forced march to the left on the orders of its president, Julius Nyerere. Business, industry, commerce, education, and agriculture are all being vigorously shaken up and prodded toward stricter accordance with the policy of *Ujamaa*—literally "familyhood," but freely translated as socialism.

Tanzania is one of the few states on the continent that has as its leader a genuine man of ideals, one sometimes wryly imagined by Europeans as being something of a saint. Nyerere claims that only by devotion to the lonely doctrine of self-reliance can the semblance of independence be transformed into a living reality. Nor has he ever been in doubt as to the kind of society he wanted to see created in his country: At the time of independence, he said, "We determined to build a country in which all her citizens were

[2] From "Atlantic Report: Tanzania." *Atlantic.* 219:32-8. Je. '67. Copyright © 1967 by The Atlantic Monthly Company, Boston, Mass. 02116. Reprinted with permission.

equal: where there is no division into rulers and ruled, rich and poor, educated and illiterate, those in distress and those in comfort."

Other men have mouthed more or less these same words in a mood of emotional ecstasy induced by watching the national flag flutter for the first time in the wind of change; few expected to treat them very seriously. Tanzania's president insists on unimpeded progress toward utopia. But he is not there yet, nor, after recent events, does he seem either the saint or the miracle worker he was once imagined to be.

An Easy Birth

The country over which Nyerere rules as president is large, poor, and backward. But it has certain advantages over comparable African states. There are only ten million people to be spread over its 360,000 square miles, so scarcity of land is no problem. Except for occasional drought in one or another district, the soil can produce enough food for the population once it is efficiently worked. Local production is primarily agricultural, but Tanzania's balance of trade is favorable; its exports total £64 million, and its imports total only £40 million.

Although there are 120 tribes, there are no major tribal problems, thanks to a British decision to make (coastal) Swahili—a mixture of Bantu and Arabic—the language of instruction in schools. Swahili is now the lingua franca of the whole country, thus enormously simplifying problems of administration and increasing Tanzania's sense of nationhood. Finally, independence was an easy birth, achieved without violent rebellion against the colonial British regime, and the nation became a one-party state.

But there is the other side: the per capita income is only £21— $58—a year. One third of all children die before they are five years old. Kwashiorkor, the protein-deficiency disease which swells the belly, dulls the eye, and leads to permanent mental retardation if not swiftly treated, is widespread. One half of the adult working population, whether on the land or in urban communities, doesn't get enough to eat and so can't function efficiently. European grumbles that it takes "three Africans to do the work of one European" are frequently true: a diet of tea and starch produces remarkably little energy.

First there was mainland Tanganyika, then in 1961 independent Tanganyika, and in 1962 the republic of Tanganyika. In 1964 came union with its offshore neighbor, the island republic of Zanzibar, following a rebellion of Zanzibar Africans against their ruling Arab aristocracy. The new nation renamed itself Tanzania.

The president of the new federation, forty-five . . . [in 1967], had been in his youth the first black Tanganyikan to go to a British university: Julius Nyerere gained his M.A. at Edinburgh. There he wrote his first pamphlet (unpublished). It was on the race problem in East Africa and indicated a rare breadth of vision at a time when his people were subjected to so rigid a discrimination that they were not even allowed to use the same door as Europeans when they visited a doctor progressive enough to treat them privately at all.

We appeal to all the people of Tanganyika [he wrote as a student at Edinburgh] to regard themselves as ordinary citizens; to preach no divine right of Europeans, no divine right of Indians and no divine right of Africans either. We are all Tanganyikans and all East Africans. The race quarrel is a stupid quarrel; it can be a very tragic quarrel but if we all make up our minds to live like ordinary sort of fellows and not to think that we were especially designed by the Creator to be masters and others specially designed to be hewers of wood and drawers of water, we will make East Africa a very happy country for everybody.

Racial equality became fundamental to Nyerere's political philosophy. And although on his return home he founded the Tanganyika African National Union (TANU) as an exclusively African organization, he insisted that this was only a temporary expedient necessary to arm Africans with the self-confidence to manage their own affairs. Even before independence, his point having been made, the party opened its ranks to all races. Today, any official position is theoretically open to any citizen, regardless of his race. There is a former British national as minister for agriculture, an Asian as minister for finance, and a former Anglo-American, Marion Lady Chesham, originally from Philadelphia, sitting in the House of Representatives. But behind the facade of official banishment of racialism, the reality of it persists.

Outward Harmony

As the independence movement gathered momentum, Nyerere began to spell out his blueprint for the future. Not only should Tanganyika be nonracial, it should be founded on the tribal principles of traditional African society which he called *Ujamaa*—familyhood, or African socialism. This differed from traditional socialism in that it did not have its roots in the class struggle but grew out of the ideal of sharing everything that was available.

Capitalism and exploitation [he declared again and again] were unknown in Africa before the coming of the colonialists, and they should not be accepted as natural in an independent Tanganyika since they are totally foreign to African ways of thinking. In our traditional African society we were individuals within the community. We took care of the community, and the community took care of us. We neither needed nor wished to exploit our fellow men.

He was at one with other African leaders in calling for nonalignment and independence from the main power blocs.

We have [he said in his independence address to the United Nations] entered a world riven by ideological dissension. We are anxious to keep out of these disputes and anxious to see that the nations of the continent are not used as pawns in conflicts which often do not concern them at all.

Inevitably, "nonalignment" occasionally meant collisions with the West. Large sums of West German aid, for example, were lost when Nyerere refused it if the price was a reversal of the decision to permit East Germany to open an unofficial consulate general; there was a rupture of relations with Britain which resulted in the freezing of a £7.5 million loan.

But on the whole, Tanzania seemed by the beginning of . . . [1967] to be a self-respecting country where Africans, Asians, and Europeans apparently lived together in outward harmony. The Tanzanians seemed serious-minded, honest, and rather humorless; those who looked for a sense of purpose in an African country found it in Tanzania. Even the foreign business community was beginning to have confidence in the avowedly leftist president and was recommending Tanzania as "safe" for investment.

Shades of Racialism

There were problems, of course, and to probing foreign observers the main one seemed to be the officially nonexistent but festering racial animosity. This would spurt up occasionally in administrative decisions (from which there was no appeal) to deport Europeans heard commenting impolitely on either the country or its inhabitants. One young teacher was sent back to Britain for muttering snappishly under her breath when annoyed by an example of bureaucratic inefficiency, "This is a crazy country."

It also manifested itself in outbursts in the press against Asian "bloodsuckers" and "economic bedbugs" who allegedly held uncooperative and anti-African attitudes.

Do not the Asians [wrote one complaining reader of the *Nationalist* . . .] still live in exclusive communities and meet in temples only to backbite the African? Do they not still continue to use foul means to destroy cooperative societies and make sure money circulates only among themselves? Do they not use all sorts of deplorable means to make sure they drain the country of its hard earned currency?

African feelings, although bitter, could be understood. With trade still largely in Asian hands and Europeans the chief spenders, a situation existed which bred resentment, envy, and helpless fury.

This distance between the official word on racialism and the fact of its existence has not greatly preoccupied the president since independence. He has had other concerns. Although outsiders saw Tanzania making solid and steady progress, for Nyerere . . . [recent] years have brought a dragging feeling of disillusion. He has watched the gap between the few "haves" and the many "have-nots" grow larger instead of smaller as the number of educated Africans in well-paying government jobs increased. Foreign aid has dwindled. Increased production of primary products has brought few benefits because of lower prices on world markets for Tanzania's exports and higher prices for its imports.

Across the continent, Nyerere saw one African government after another topple and turn to military rule, the foundation of civilian authority eaten away by corruption. And he had to accept the impotence of Africans to help the black Rhodesians against Smith. [See Section V, below.] "There is," he said glumly after an unsuccessful OAU meeting at the end of last year, "a devil abroad in Africa."

Down With Elitism

Particularly distressing to him was what he felt to be the diminishing idealism of his own people. Nyerere with his conception of an indigenous *Ujamaa* is, on the face of it, a supporter of neither Soviet nor Chinese communism—communism, he says, sacrifices the individual to the state in the same way as fascism does. But the fact is that he came back from a visit to China in 1965 bubbling with enthusiasm for Chinese frugality and self-denial, which he may have confused with poverty, and proceeded to translate his impressions of China into a government-run Tanzanian revolution along lines at least superficially Maoist.

There are hardly any private cars in China [he said in a radio broadcast on his return] and people go to work by bus or bicycle. Government officials too use cars only when it is really necessary for their job—and then the cars are small and cheap ones. Workers who do not need to spend all their money on food, clothing, and housing do not buy a lot of unnecessary things just because they would be nice to have or because someone else has them; they lend their money to the government instead so that more investment, more education, and more health facilities can be provided.... This attitude we have to adopt too.

Nevertheless, the trend continued. Almost overnight a governmental middle class seemed to be springing up. Ministers and senior party officials, most of whose illiterate parents scratched for subsistence somewhere up-country, were building houses for rent at exorbitant sums to foreign diplomats, investing in commercial ventures—a favorite was the purchase of oil trucks for the run between Tanzania and Zambia—or accepting directorships in European companies anxious to have an African or two on the board.

What hurt Nyerere most were signs that the younger generation of intellectuals rejected his doctrine that public money spent on their education (secondary and university education are free) must be repaid by a lifetime of dedicated service to the nation. His frustration broke out publicly . . . [in October 1966] when university students protested compulsory national service. This, they claimed, was a waste of their talents; national service ought to conscript only the uneducated masses, with whom students ought not to have to mix. They marched in procession to the state house to tell the president so. A furious Nyerere had them taken off the campus under armed guard the following day, and forbade them to return for two years. More than three hundred students were affected, or about two thirds of the university student body—a desperately needed future class of lawyers, economists, or administrators.

The country was stunned; and reeled again when the president announced that in a further bid to halt "elitism" he was cutting his own salary by 10 per cent and all civil servants' salaries as well. For good measure, ministers would no longer have cars provided for them by the government, but would have to drive their own.

Two Tanzanias

This was only the beginning. Nyerere set off at Christmas [1966] on a tour of the country's regions, deriding farmers who left the work to their wives while they dozed in the sun sodden with *pombe,* the locally brewed liquor. He told them to build their own roads, dig their own ditches, and put up their own schools instead of begging for everything from the government. Privately, he was pondering the specter of Tanzania dividing into two countries: that of the rural poor, still steeped in witchcraft, unable to read or write, not yet part of a cash economy; and the indifferent, relatively affluent educated minority who were taking over not only the jobs but the mental attitudes of their former colonial masters.

At the end of his six-week tour the president revealed his new hard line to a national executive meeting of TANU in the town of Arusha, and on February 5, [1967] the Arusha Declaration was made known to the nation. It reiterated that Tanzania was pledged to socialism and self-reliance. Only socialism could lead to a society where "there are no exploiters and no exploited," and only through self-reliance could real independence be won: "There is no country in the world which has progressed and developed by relying on foreign aid," said Nyerere. "Indeed, those countries which have pinned their hopes on foreign aid are sinking lower and lower in development."

In theory this was nothing new, and it had in fact become tedious through repetition; but this time Nyerere proceeded to act on his rhetoric quickly. The Arusha Declaration announced that "no TANU or government leader was henceforth to be associated with the practice of capitalism or feudalism," that he was not to hold shares in any company or be a director of any company, or receive more than one salary, or own a house in which he did not live. Twenty-four hours later came an announcement of nationalization of the banks, and there began a whirlwind week of crisis at the end of which eight major flour mills as well as the most important export-import firms and some large industrial concerns had all been taken over by the government.

Nor was Nyerere's revolution finished even then. He turned next to a radical revision of the educational system. Although the curriculum had been made more relevant to local needs than it was under British rule, education in Tanzania was still geared to the achievement of as high an academic standard as possible. Children in Tanzania who fail to get into secondary school, as the vast majority do, have very little choice but to scratch a living from the land. Nyerere's new proposals call for the complete reorientation of the school curriculum toward the needs of these children who will not be going on to secondary school and for whom an agricultural training is the only realistic one. Schools, he said, should become self-sufficient communities growing their own food and cultivating their own land; and while the bright child would still have every opportunity to go on to a higher education, the less bright would learn to be a useful member of an agricultural community.

Revolution or Standstill?

Nyerere has risked the pace of his country's development before —by his attitude toward offers of aid, by his dismissal of the university students—but this time it is possible that he may have brought development to a standstill. The immediate result of the nationalization measures has been a complete stagnation of business. Asians, disturbed by a xenophobic campaign by the minister of home affairs to round up and deport all noncitizens, feel no confidence in their future and are putting very little money into their businesses. So stocks are running down.

Equally serious in the long run may be the shamed resentment felt by government and party officials at the president's austerity campaign. They have struggled hard for their education, and are thrilled with the material benefits it has brought them. They don't see why their enjoyment of their new way of life does any harm to the peasants. Nor do they relish Nyerere's new habit of haranguing against "intellectuals" as potential traitors whom the "imperialists will attempt to use to topple progressive governments."

As for reaction abroad, the hasty and totally unprepared manner in which nationalization was rushed through wrecked business confidence in Tanzania. There is little money in Dar es Salaam to pay those whose companies have been nationalized, whatever the president may in all sincerity say about intending compensation to be "full and fair." And while Nyerere's personal honesty and integrity are not doubted, his declining sense of realism is viewed with alarm.

Moreover, no amount of self-help, admirable in itself, can make up for the capital investment needed for development. It is now questionable whether much at all will be forthcoming. Tanzania may therefore be moving into a period of stagnant if righteous isolation—driven back on itself not only as a consequence of the reaction to its policies abroad, but equally as much because Nyerere does not believe contact with the wicked world can solve any of his country's problems.

He said in an address to the FAO [Food and Agriculture Organization of the United Nations] in 1963: "Disparities between the rich and the poor nations are bound to get bigger just as the runt of the litter always goes hungry." The solution he tentatively proposed then was the withdrawal of the underdeveloped countries from contact with the rest of the world, although he admitted that

any such action would be "a backward step . . . which might lead
to the deliberate development of a jingoistic hostility towards the
wealthy minority." Nevertheless, he felt the cost might one day
have to be met "to defeat the poverty, both objective and relative,
which now oppresses us." A continuation of the present combination of "aid" and "free international competition," he said, would
never do that.

It looks today as if Nyerere is preparing for his prophecies to
come true, at least in his own country. For the rest of East Africa,
nervously watching Tanzania, Nyerere's ideas seem to have little
appeal. And there is always the possibility that Nyerere may himself fail, as a result of asking too much of his own people. But it is
hard for any challenger to oppose a man who never, morally, puts
a foot wrong.

UGANDA UNDER A. MILTON OBOTE [3]

Uganda is an enchanted country, at once equatorial and salu-
brious, situated some several thousand feet above the level of the
sea, a land of grassy hills, glinting lakes and crested cranes, of the
sources of the Nile and the Mountains of the Moon. It is, like the
other nations of East Africa, a British invention, and one of which
the British have some reason to be proud, for they ruled it rather
well from the day they imposed their protectorate in 1894 until they
made the country independent . . . [in 1962].

Lord Lugard, soldier and adventurer, created Uganda partly out
of the Bantu kingdoms of Buganda, Bunyoro, Ankole and Toro—
all but one of which have, in their anomalous African way, kept
their tribal monarchies intact, even though the modern Uganda
which comprises them is officially a unitary state. In this epoch of
galloping egalitarianism such kingships should have the right to be
retained for the resonance of their nomenclature if for nothing else.
How many hierarchies elsewhere can rival a Sir Charles Godfrey
Gasyonga II, Rubambansi the Mugabe of Ankole? Or a Sir George
David Kamurasi Rukidi III, Rukirabasaija the Mukama of Toro?

[3] Article, "Making of a President, Uganda Style," by Edward R. F. Sheehan, an American journalist and novelist who writes frequently about Africa. New York *Times Magazine.* p 36-7+. Ja. 22, '67. Copyright © 1967 by The New York Times Company. Reprinted by permission.

Or a Sir Tito Gafabusa Winyi IV, the Mukama of Bunyoro? One might even mention His Highness Sir Edward Frederick Mutesa II, K.B.E., the Kabaka of Buganda—"King Freddie" to his friends— were it not for his recent and very involuntary retirement.

In fact, if we intend to talk about Uganda, we can hardly avoid mentioning either the Kabaka of Buganda or the exceedingly unceremonious circumstances of his deposition. A gregarious, easygoing gentleman, the Kabaka sat on a lion-headed throne in robes of almost papal splendor, an object of intense reverence among his people, who are Uganda's richest and most advanced, though they embody but a seventh of the country's total population of about seven million. In view of his kingdom's resources, it was understandably disturbing to the central government when, last May [1966], the Kabaka's legislature ordered the central government out of Bugandan territory forthwith. Indeed, since the national capital, Kampala, is situated in the very heart of Buganda, it is not surprising that President A. Milton Obote considered the eviction notice an act of rebellion. Thus did a prolonged war of nerves between Uganda's two most prominent personalities—the Kabaka and Obote—escalate into a final confrontation.

On May 23, much of Buganda rose up in revolt against the central government. Police stations were put to the torch, a policeman in one was burned alive, some civilians were killed, roadblocks were erected, communications were cut. Mobs of Baganda (as the tribesmen of Buganda are called) began to rampage about; some wielded *pangas* [machetes], others had firearms. A few of those arrested with firearms confessed they had obtained them from the Kabaka's great-walled, silver-domed palace atop Mengo Hill outside Kampala. President Obote declared a state of emergency, and, so it is said, was moved to quote a maxim popular among African revolutionaries: "When an old society is pregnant with a new one, the only midwife is force." He ordered the Uganda army to surround the Kabaka's palace.

At dawn of May 24, the army (possibly exceeding Obote's instructions) launched a heavy assault on the palace, where hundreds of Baganda had gathered to defend their ruler against just such a danger. After twelve hours of savage combat, interrupted at one point by a heavy rainstorm but costing in the end perhaps two or three hundred lives, the government troops overran the palace and seized a large quantity of illegal arms and ammunition.

In the meanwhile, the Kabaka himself had managed an escape which has already become part of the mythology of his people. In his own version of the events, recounted later in London, he jumped from the high wall of the palace—and hailed a taxi which happened to be passing by. ("My brother, Prince Henry, was less fortunate," the Kabaka has written. "Prince Henry found no taxi and had to queue for a bus.") The Kabaka then related a heart-rending tale of his own trek for several weeks and many hundreds of miles through the bush, forests and savanna of Uganda, living on wild berries and sweet potatoes, sleeping in thorn thickets. Eventually, he says, he reached the Congo and then hitchhiked to Burundi, whence he flew to his present exile in London.

The Kabaka placed full blame for his downfall on the misdeeds of Dr. Obote.

He considered me a rival, a fact which might surprise those who think of me as a playboy monarch, gay King Freddie, late of Cambridge University and the Brigade of Guards. Uganda is fast becoming a totalitarian, one-party police state. Milton Obote is an intelligent man, and an able one, but in power and seeking power he has learned all the wrong lessons. He has become a schemer; his mind dwells always on plots and plotting, and he suspects everyone else is the same. It was not always so. He once had a strain of humanity which now seems to have become lost. . . .

Tribe and Tradition

The collision of the Kabaka and President Obote dramatizes the clash between tribal tradition and the new nationalism that is raging throughout all of Africa. History is the mother of irony, and it is interesting that the Kabaka of Buganda, whose ancestors were noted for the savage speed with which they dispatched all suspected rivals, should now himself become the victim of precautionary violence. Indeed, unless we understand something of the history of Buganda, the country's most recent convulsions make little sense.

In contrast to the highly civilized contemporary Kabaka, his namesake and ancestor, Mutesa I, who ruled Buganda at the time of its first penetration by the British a century ago, was (in Alan Moorehead's phrase) "a savage and bloodthirsty monster." On becoming king he instantly burned alive some sixty of his brothers (which was regarded as a normal precaution against rebellion), and on one particularly horrendous day he had two thousand victims tortured and burned at the stake as an offering to the spirit of his father, Suna.

Nevertheless, Mutesa was a gifted ruler. In fact, for centuries before the coming of the British, the Baganda had belied the myth that, left to themselves, untouched by Western civilization, Africans could not rise above the most primitive forms of human society. Before having any contact with the outside world, they had achieved a culture well in advance of any other south of the Sahara; though they were illiterate and their religion was a barbarous witchcraft, they were accomplished in weaving, music and architecture.

Following the imposition of the protectorate, the British used the Baganda to wage wars of pacification against many of the twenty-five or thirty other tribes in Uganda. As a reward, Buganda was granted a privileged status together with portions of other tribal kingdoms. Its system of tribal administration was extended by the British over the whole protectorate. After World War II, Britain's hesitant efforts to develop Uganda into a democratic, integrated nation constantly stumbled over the special rights previously granted to Buganda. The intensely tribalistic Baganda wanted nothing to do with a united Uganda, and in our own time they have, under the most recent Kabaka, ceaselessly intrigued for their independence as a separate nation. Before Britain granted Uganda independence in 1962, Buganda made several attempts to secede from the rest of the country. It took a most delicately balanced federal constitution to delay the day of judgment that finally came this year with the uprising of the Baganda and then the central government's reprisal against the royal palace. With that reprisal, nationalism seemed to triumph over tribalism; President Obote seemed to have vanquished his great antagonist. But the Baganda will not soon forget the dishonoring of their king—nor can anyone insure that, despite their present mood of impotence, they will not one day rise up again to inflict on President Obote the traditional vengeance of the Mutesas.

Obote's Background

What sort of man is this who toppled King Freddie from his throne? Apollo Milton Obote was born in a mud hut, sometime in 1924—he knows neither the month nor the day—in the small village of Akakoro on Lake Kwania, Lango District, in northern Uganda. He is the third of nine children born to Stanley Opeto, a minor chieftain, and his wife Pulisikira. (Opeto was polygamous and had three other wives.)

Obote is a Lango, one of the northern Nilotic tribes, tribal origins always being significant in the career of any African politician. Even today a visit to his birthplace reveals much of the man: The crooked thatch-roofed huts of his childhood are gone, but nearby, amidst tall green grass and flat-topped acacia trees, identical dwellings have replaced them. His elderly father inhabits a neat, painted mud hut to this day, and has journeyed to the capital, Kampala, only once in his lifetime.

It is not true that I began life as a poor boy, as so many say [Dr. Obote remarked in a conversation I had with him recently in Kampala]. I was born of a ruling family. My grandfather, great-grandfather and great-great-grandfather were all rulers. But the story of my having been a shepherd, and a goatherd, is true. My father wanted to keep me near him. All my brothers and sisters went to school, but I remained at home with my father. Odd as it might appear, I took this as a sign of my father's love for me. I used to spend hours a day tending to my sheep, cattle and goats—all alone. I started school when I was twelve years old.

Obote's academic history is not a glittering one; he joins Sir Winston Churchill on the list of dropouts of distinction. He was discharged from more than one secondary school for failing to meet required standards, and at Makerere University College in Kampala he withdrew (but was not expelled) after two years.

I left Makerere because I decided I wanted to practice either law or politics [Obote says]. I was offered a chance to study law by an American university, but the Uganda government (that is, the British) turned me down because they said that American law was no good for this country.

Then they refused me a place at Gordon Memorial College at Khartoum because they said I could not make up my mind where or what I wanted to study. So I gave up and took some correspondence courses instead.

Obote's attitude toward the British today seems to reflect the classical compound of envy, reverence and resentment so common among his generation of African intelligentsia.

His relatively scant formal education—his failure either to achieve distinction as a scholar at home or to attend a university in England or America—has unquestionably marked Obote psychologically and has given him what one of his critics claims is "a painful inferiority complex which he seeks to conceal in various pretentious ways." These considerations may help to explain some of the interesting, and by no means obnoxious, poses which Obote strikes as president today—the conscious and somewhat strained elegance of his conversational English (despite a very difficult accent), his obvious disdain of native costumes, the impeccability and deliberate good taste of his British-cut wardrobe, the title of "Doctor" that he brandishes before his name. His "doctorate" is purely an encomium, an honorary LL.D. awarded to him by Long Island University during a visit to America, and most probably arranged by the State Department.

Rise to Political Power

At twenty-six, not long after leaving Makerere, Obote took a job in Kenya as a common laborer at a sugar works, for about $3 a month. "I had become interested in the trade-union movement, and I decided that the best way to learn about trade unionism was at the bottom," he says. He drifted in Kenya from one humble job to another—laborer, clerk, salesman—engaging (despite British displeasure) in union organizing, and learning something of African street politics as a founder-member of the Kenya African Union.

In 1957, having returned home, Obote was named by the Lango district council as a representative in the national legislative council in Kampala, the precursor of the present parliament. From that moment, his rise to prominence and power was phenomenally swift, and he soon became a skillful craftsman in the black Byzantium of Ugandan tribal politics.

Though he entered parliament as a member of the Uganda National Congress (and soon became its head), he broke away from the UNC following a factional dispute and founded the Uganda People's Congress (UPC) in 1960, with himself as president. A boycott by Buganda removed many more experienced leaders from parliament, and in 1961 Obote emerged as leader of the opposition. In the following year, he led his party to victory in the national elections which preceded Uganda's full independence.

As prime minister, Obote played a major role in framing the Ugandan constitution at a conference in London on the eve of independence. In his bargaining, he was forced to make full allowances for Bugandan particularism; the ultimate independence constitution granted Buganda a large measure of self-rule and seemed to perpetuate the kingdom's special position as first among equals.

In fact, Obote's party, though the largest, lacked a majority in parliament. The second-largest faction was the predominantly Roman Catholic Democratic party; the balance of power was held by the radical Bagandan Kabaka Yekka (Kabaka Only) party. To govern, Obote was obliged to forge an unnatural and exceedingly uneasy coalition with the Kabaka Yekka—a coalition that attempted to accommodate two totally contradictory visions of Uganda's future. Even then, it was no secret that Obote aspired to a unified country which would eventually adopt a unitary constitution within a one-party state.

As a means of integrating Buganda with the rest of the nation, Obote—with great difficulty—persuaded his party to accept the Kabaka as president of the whole country. It did not take Obote and the Kabaka terribly long to have a falling out. But by offers of government patronage and other means, Obote began to lure MP's of the other two parties into his own UPC. When he had a clear majority, he broke off the coalition. By mid-1965, the country seemed on the verge of becoming a one-party state.

Then the UPC ran into trouble. The cabinet began to split up along tribal lines. One clique was identified with Obote and labeled "the northerners"; the other, labeled "the Bantu faction," was composed mostly of southerners. By the beginning of 1966, tribal, religious, ideological, factional and personal disputes within the UPC became so serious that the party appeared on the point of disintegration. From without, Buganda's hostility to the central government was renewed with growing force.

1966 Crisis

A major crisis was inevitable, and it exploded at the beginning of . . . February [1966]. Obote left Kampala for a fortnight's tour of his home area in the north. Hardly was he out of the capital when the cabinet joined parliament in accusing him and three associates of corruption and of plotting to overthrow the constitution.

Kampala reeked with rumors of coup and countercoup; whispers whirled of mysterious troop movements; ministers vanished from their ministries. But though his government seemed about to topple with an ignominious thud, the prime minister did not panic. He calmly continued his tour of the north, dedicating schools and addressing throngs of his own people, carefully considering his next moves and—given his character—probably plotting fifty steps ahead of his enemies.

Then he returned to Kampala and immediately seized the initiative. He publicly denied the charges against him, and, surprisingly, prevailed upon the cabinet to create an impartial and irreproachable commission of inquiry composed of three distinguished judges from Kenya and Tanzania. The testimony at the hearings was tortuous and contradictory. One key witness disappeared, and many questions—such as the fate of some smuggled Congolese gold—remained unanswered. But the hearings produced no conclusive evidence against Obote or his supporters.

Meanwhile, Obote was maneuvering to regroup his forces and consolidate his power. At a cabinet meeting in late February, police burst in, and—despite some understandable kicks and screams—dragged the five dissident "Bantu" ministers (whom Obote accused of having plotted with the Kabaka) off to imprisonment in the north. Obote then announced that, to avert an antigovernment army coup, he was temporarily assuming all powers, suspending the constitution and dismissing the Kabaka from his office as president. The rest of the cabinet rallied to the prime minister and he entrusted effective control of the army to a friend and fellow northerner, Idi Amin.

On April 15, Obote suddenly convened parliament and informed the members that they were sitting as a constituent assembly to pass on a new constitution. The document proclaimed Uganda henceforth a unitary state—depriving the Kingdom of Buganda of both its federal status and many of its entrenched privileges. The roar of Uganda air force jets could be heard overhead, armed troops gazed down from the galleries; the Speaker forthwith called for the vote. Not surprisingly, parliament chose to ratify. Prime Minister Obote was promptly sworn in as Uganda's new president—an office which he had taken care to provide with very strong powers—and the chief justice took an oath of allegiance to the new constitution, thereby intimating that its legality would be upheld in the courts. Despite its highly unorthodox manner of presentation, Obote's constitution retained many provisions of the old one, nor did it deal a deathblow to the system of checks and balances.

There followed the disastrous decision by the Buganda legislature to order the central government out of Buganda, and Obote's angry rejoinder in dispatching government troops to the palace of the Kabaka.

Obote's Aims—and Style

President Obote appears obsessed with his private vision of becoming a nation builder, the acknowledged founding father of a united and integrated Uganda, and the architect of a major and lasting transformation of its feudal society. As yet, he enjoys neither the prestige nor the personal fame of East Africa's other two presidents—Jomo Kenyatta of Kenya and Dr. Julius Nyerere of Tanzania—but he probably surpasses both of them as a tactician and as a pure political animal who possesses an almost mystical understanding of the mechanics and sources of power. He does not inspire the awe or reverence that Kenyatta's charismatic history commands in Kenya. Nor, despite his intelligence and omnivorous reading habits, can he claim to possess the intellectual brilliance of Nyerere, but then, neither is he burdened with the excessive introspection, diffidence and indecisiveness which so often seem to have immobilized the president of Tanzania.

In the misty forest of Ugandan tribal politics, however, Obote has proved himself to be a maneuverer whose foresight and cunning have invariably overturned the most ingenious stratagems of his enemies. When his political fortunes were at their lowest ebb, and just as he appeared to be losing his grip, not only did he surprise his opponents by creating the commission of inquiry, but he took the brilliant gamble of assuring that its composition was beyond his political control, free to scrutinize his personal probity as it pleased. Then he turned the attention of the country from the debate over his honesty to the controversy over his new constitution.

In their repeated confrontations, Obote has consistently outwitted the Kabaka, who never really had the stomach for the power game in the first place. The Kabaka was under pressure from his own people to prove that he was running Buganda, and pushed by foolish advisers to take untenable positions from which there was no retreat.

Despite some lingering suspicions of his probity, even Obote's severe critics concede that avarice is not one of his primary motivations. He has not enriched his family, nor does he live luxuriously himself. He has yet to move to the presidential mansion from the more modest prime minister's residence, where he lives with his third wife, Miria—a Baganda tribeswoman—and some of his children. He is a notoriously frugal eater with a bad stomach, and at public gatherings he does little more than pick at his food.

Like other leaders of his type, Obote has surrounded himself with a cabinet now composed for the most part of nonentities. Well aware of the limitations of his own lieutenants, and apparently convinced that he is the one man in Uganda who can do things properly, he finds it difficult to delegate authority and reserves virtually all major decisions to himself, determining even such matters as agricultural or mineral policy over the heads of the ministers concerned. He is of course careful not to permit any rivals to his power, and each time he leaves the country he deputizes a different minister. He watches the army very closely, as well he should; he has been purging Bantu officers, replacing them with northerners, and giving the new leadership pretty much what it wants. But what will happen if one day the army decides that Obote is not giving enough?

Obote is extremely moody. He oscillates between congeniality and belligerency. At times he rages at his ministers as if they were schoolboys. People who have argued with him say that he has an irrational hatred of being challenged. His eyes flame; at times he becomes violent and, some believe, unbalanced; when he is caught in this temper there is no reasoning with him. In the past, moreover, he has displayed not only a certain tendency toward deceit but a highly developed talent for rabble-rousing. He is, one acquaintance says, "congenitally suspicious—ready to believe anything."

Relations With the United States

His suspicions used to turn rather often against the United States, but his relations with Washington have improved remarkably in recent months, due in no small measure to the arrival of Henry Stebbins as American ambassador.

The Soviet influence in Kampala is much stronger than the Chinese. As for his own ideology, Obote says: "I have none, except pragmatism." Nor is he necessarily as dazzled by the doctrines of the one-party state as he once appeared to be. Now that there are few more than a handful of opposition members left in parliament, he is said to believe that "any majority of more than fifty is dangerous." He is apparently disillusioned because the lop-sided predominance of his own party has invited division and decay, not to mention subversion, nepotism, inefficiency, apathy and the arrogance that accompanies too much power.

Obote is now said to recognize the need for a free and effective opposition as he casts his eye across Africa and discerns the general failure to devise workable alternatives to the stimulus of rival parties.

Despite all the high-flown theories propounded for Africa by Western liberals, the single-party state does not necessarily represent all of the people or even a substantial part of them; neither does it guarantee a stable government nor a liberation from tribalism. Even in Tanzania, Dr. Nyerere felt obliged to put up rival candidates within his single-party system to provide his people with a genuine choice during their most recent national elections.

Does this mean that President Obote will allow early, free elections to submit his new constitution and his own popularity to the judgment of his people? He has been vague about that.

Benedicto Kiwanuka, the president of the Democratic party (the once-upon-a-time opposition), who was chief minister of Uganda before independence, is much more definite.

Obote has become a dictator. If the Kabaka should test his deposition in the courts and win, Obote might decide to imitate Nkrumah and depose the judges.

I don't hold any brief for the Kabaka—I had my own battles with him when I was chief minister—but we mean to have free elections and we mean to put an end to Obote's dictatorship, and I invite you to believe me.

What Obote Believes

My encounter with Dr. Obote himself came in his modest office in the modernistic parliament building in Kampala. He was faultlessly tailored in a dark business suit; black, small-buckled shoes; a tie emblazoned with a tiny, crested crane, the symbolic bird of Uganda. He smoked incessantly; on occasion he would reach out from his chair to finger his quilted walking stick. Leisurely, and sometimes eloquently, he gave voice to his convictions.

The violent events of last May? "I'm ruined and heartbroken by what happened. I feel that Uganda, our precious pearl, has been soiled."

African corruption: "It stems simply from the failure of the corrupted politicians to appreciate their role in society."

The CIA: "I'm not supposed to know that they're around. I'm afraid of them. Probably they spy on their own ambassadors."

Red China: "I told Chou En-lai that if I found his men working against our government, I would close their embassy. I have a lot of problems here, and I would like to solve them in my own way. I have no need, thank you, for Chinese solutions."

Personal ambition? "I've thought of nothing except to serve the people. When my party won the general election just before independence, I was in my constituency at Lira, 130 miles from the capital. The first thing I did was to jump into a tribal dance. I had no idea at all that at that time I should be thinking about forming a government. Then a police car came, and we thought it was to stop the dancing. An officer got out. . . ."

"A Ugandan?"

"No, he was British. He saluted me and his words were: 'Sir, there is a message for you from the governor. . . .' "

Dusk began to invade the president's parliamentary office. His voice grew low, almost drowsy, but it did not seem that he wished just yet to terminate his reminiscence. We were in the middle of modern Kampala, but even in that marble building we could hear the croakings of the African twilight and the distant calling of exotic birds. The president's skin glowed like a black boot; at the nape of his neck he pulled absently—dreamily—at his long, coarse hair; he surrendered himself to a great nostalgia.

I faintly suspected that I was being treated to some sort of performance—and yet I was moved. I wondered: Is he an Ataturk, a Machiavelli or just a good actor, this goatherd in the Savile Row suit? Or perhaps all of that at once? Would he survive to consummate the building of his nation, or would he be intercepted by the ancient justice of the Kabakas?

This ambition, this "will to power" that you speak of, never bothered me at all [he said]. When I was a herdboy watching my flocks I thought about my brothers and sisters at school, and at times during the holidays they were very nasty. At times they even called me a great fool because I did not know how to read or write, and because I was not at school. At the same time, my uncle, the elder brother of my father, was a big chief, and my father was a subcounty chief. I knew that neither my father nor my uncle had gone to school, yet their work was to look after the affairs of men. I therefore turned my cattle, sheep and goats into human beings, and I tried—so to speak—to govern them.

"Was it then that you began to glimpse what you are today?" I asked.

At times I tried to talk to them, and to pretend that I was myself a chief governing men [he said]. But, since they were animals, I had to care for them. In the afternoons, when I used to drive them home, I had a big problem of doing things in such a manner that some would not run too fast and leave me behind with the others. Perhaps you can see what my position was? They were animals. I needed their cooperation. . . .

III. ECONOMIC PROBLEMS AND PROSPECTS

EDITOR'S INTRODUCTION

For every newly emerging country, the real test of success seems to lie in the economy. Spiritual values may be hailed, political forms fiercely contested. But in the end, it is the material well-being of citizens that seems to count the most. Perhaps that is one reason why most governments in newly independent states play such pronounced economic roles. Perhaps that is why socialism, in one form or another, is the economic system most widely adopted.

Thus it is in Kenya, Tanzania, and Uganda. Each of these economies wears a Socialist label, though each has its own distinctive features. Kenya's brand of socialism is pragmatic and easy-going. Foreign capitalists are welcome to invest. Western influence is strong, and Kenya's economy is moving forward at a brisk pace. In Tanzania socialism is much more ideologically oriented, much more doctrinaire. A sweeping round of nationalization early in 1967 tightened President Nyerere's economic control. Foreign influence is viewed with suspicion and distrust. Bootstrap progress, based upon self-help and communal sacrifice, is the goal. Uganda walks a middle course. She, too, is undergoing some belt-tightening in the midst of her second five-year plan. But Uganda, economically the weakest of the three countries under study, is working hard to attract foreign investments and raise the level of her poorest citizens.

The economic headway being made by these three nations is the subject of this section. The first two articles discuss Tanzania's plans and prospects. After a general survey by the Foreign Information Service of the First National City Bank of New York, a specialist in East African politics discusses the merits and defects of Nyerere's Arusha Declaration on economic reform. The next two articles give a generally optimistic view of Kenya's economic progress. In the last two articles, the development problems facing Uganda are discussed.

TANZANIA'S ECONOMY: A PROFILE [1]

Capital: Dar es Salaam

Area: 364,000 square miles (larger than Texas and Oklahoma combined) of which Zanzibar: 1,020 square miles

Population: 10.3 million, of which Zanzibar: 330,000

Principal Tanganyika Exports (1964): sisal (31 per cent), coffee (16 per cent), cotton (14 per cent), diamonds (10 per cent)

Principal Zanzibar Exports (1964): cloves and clove oil (80 per cent), coconut products (18 per cent)

United States Aid Investment Guarantees: convertibility, expropriation, war or civil disturbances, extended risk

Tanganyika is in most part a land of rolling plains and plateaus, with mountains grouped in the southwestern and northeastern corners. It contains the highest mountain in Africa, Kilimanjaro (19,565 feet) and the lowest depression, Lake Tanganyika. The average elevation is four thousand feet, resulting in a temperate climate over most of the country. Rainfall is generally low, seasonal, and variable. There are few permanent rivers except near the coast, and much of the central region is arid bush country. Compounding the scarcity of water, a thin, infertile soil makes arable land scarce; less than 10 per cent of the area is under cultivation. Tsetse fly infestation limits grazing activities.

Consequently, economic activity takes place mainly on the periphery, particularly along the coast and in the Lake Victoria basin. The population is African with the exception of about 116,000 Asians and Arabs, who control most of the trade, and 20,000 Europeans engaged in a wide range of activities.

Zanzibar, some twenty-five miles off the coast of Tanganyika, comprises three coral islands: Zanzibar, the largest; Pemba, which contains most of the clove plantations; and small, deserted Latham Island. The climate is tropical and rainy, governed by monsoons. The population is almost entirely Moslem, with Africans making up three quarters of the total, and the remainder mostly Arab.

[1] From *East and Central Africa—A Survey of Six Developing Countries.* Foreign Information Service. First National City Bank. New York. '66. p 11-14. Reprinted by permission.

Structure of the Economy

Agriculture and grazing are the mainstays of Tanganyika's economy, accounting for 80 per cent of foreign trade and 70 per cent of gross national product. GNP in 1964 was valued at $720 million, a 6 per cent increase over 1963 at current prices. Per capita GNP amounts to $72.

Zanzibar is not self-sufficient in food and has to rely on imports financed by its sales of cloves—of which it produces 80 per cent of world output—and coconut products. GDP [gross domestic product] is estimated at $34 million.

Over 90 per cent of the active population of Tanganyika is engaged in farming, mostly centered around subsistence crops. Only 10 per cent of the cultivated land is used for cash crops. Tanganyika is the world's largest producer of sisal, accounting for more than a third of the world supply. Other major export items are coffee and cotton—production of which has tripled since the 1950's. Pyrethrum, tobacco, and tea are becoming increasingly important as export crops. Hides and skins are the leading exports of the livestock industry. It is expected that soon Tanganyika will be self-sufficient in sugar.

Mining in the aggregate provides about as much foreign exchange as either coffee or cotton. Diamond production accounts for two thirds of the total mineral output. Other important mineral resources are gold, lead, copper, and mica, but many other deposits of lesser economic importance are also being exploited or are known to exist.

Half of electricity production is thermal, and the remainder hydroelectric. There are no fuels other than wood. Forests cover 12 per cent of the area, and about 40 per cent of the production of hardwoods is exported. A program of forest development and reforestation has been in effect for the past several years.

Transportation is a problem because of the distance between population centers. Despite an extensive road network, rapid motor transport is handicapped by poor surfacing and washouts. The railroads are the backbone of the transport system, branching out of the three ocean ports: Tanga, Mtwara, and Dar es Salaam. The latter serves a large area through a central line to the west and to the northwest towards Lake Victoria, where it is supplemented by lake transport.

Industry consists mainly of facilities for processing agricultural output, but has been expanding in recent years and now includes two auto assembly plants, sawmills, furniture making, cement, plastics, pharmaceuticals, and soap factories and a radio assembly plant—the first of its kind in East Africa. An oil refinery is planned for Dar es Salaam.

Foreign Trade and Payments

Tanganyika usually runs a considerable export surplus in its external trade, excluding exchanges with Kenya and Uganda. In contrast, trade with these two countries has shown a large deficit. Imports from Kenya and Uganda have amounted to about a third of total imports, and have been some five times larger than intra-area exports. The external trade surplus for 1965 contracted as drought cut sisal output and stiff competition from Brazil affected sisal prices—which fell more than 40 per cent below 1964 levels. A larger cotton crop was offset by a price dip, and excess coffee could not be sold because of a low quota imposed by the International Coffee Agreement.

The United Kingdom remains Tanganyika's major trading partner; in 1964 it took 30 per cent of Tanganyika's exports, and provided 33 per cent of its imports. The United States is the country's fourth leading customer for exports, but is the major coffee buyer, taking nearly half of production; the U.S. share of imports is small. Other trading partners outside of East Africa are West Germany, Japan, India, and Hong Kong.

Zanzibar's trade, which averages between $20 and $30 million a year—less than 10 per cent of Tanganyika's total—has been running a deficit in recent years, but in 1964 exports and imports were approximately in balance. Zanzibar's leading trade partners have been India and Indonesia; however, the country's sales to Europe have tripled since the late fifties. Reexport trade, which formerly was important, has dwindled away.

In 1965, the United Kingdom extended a $21 million interest-free loan to help cover the costs of the first two years of Tanganyika's development plan. Total U.K. financial assistance to Tanzania amounted to $20.7 million in fiscal 1964-1965, the same as in the year before. Aid has also been received from the United States, West Germany, and mainland China.

Economic Policies and Planning

Following the completion in 1964 of a $67 million plan geared towards the development of water resources, modernization of agriculture, and expansion of secondary manufacturing, Tanganyika moved on to a series of three five-year development plans. The first, in which it is now engaged, aims at the further expansion of industry and the resettlement of farmers on new irrigated land to ease overcrowding in the fertile areas, where land hunger has now become apparent. The plan calls for a $689 million investment; less than half is slated to be contributed by the government, which anticipates acquiring most of the funds needed through external borrowing. National output is expected to increase by an average of 6.7 per cent a year over the plan period.

The fully government-owned Tanganyika Development Corporation and the Tanganyika Development Finance Company Ltd. —whose capital was provided by the TDC, the Commonwealth Development Corporation, and a West German agency—provide assistance to the private sector. A foreign investment (protection) bill specifies legal guarantees for overseas investors, including compensation in case of nationalization.

Zanzibar also has a development program under way, aiming at the diversification of the economy and the expansion of tourism.

SOCIALISM—TANZANIAN STYLE [2]

Most African states profess one form of socialism or another as their philosophy of government. Tanzania is one of the few to begin making the transition from rhetoric to reality.

[2] From "Meaning of Arusha," by Martin Lowenkopf, senior research fellow at the University College, Dar es Salaam, Tanzania. *Africa Report.* 12:8-10. Mr. '67. Reprinted by permission.

In January, President Julius Nyerere made a month-long tour of rural Tanzania—the "long march," the press of the governing Tanganyika African National Union called it. On completing his journey, he convened a meeting of the TANU National Executive Committee at Arusha, a small town in the northern highlands of the country. The outcome of these deliberations, announced by Nyerere on February 5, was the Arusha Declaration, a statement of TANU's credo on socialism and economic development. Beginning the next day, in a series of moves that were as swift as they were unexpected, Nyerere nationalized the foreign-owned commercial banks, import-export firms, and insurance companies, and took a controlling interest in the larger industrial establishments and agricultural estates. He promised "full and fair" compensation to the former owners.

Nyerere had at a stroke brought his country further along the road to socialism than even former President Kwame Nkrumah had taken Ghana. Had Nyerere succumbed to Communist influence, Western journalists asked? Had, indeed, the Chinese- and East German-influenced Zanzibari tail wagged the Tanganyikan dog? From the vantage point of Dar es Salaam, it is the questions that are naïve, not, as some correspondents are fond of saying, Julius Nyerere.

A Message to "Black Capitalists"

Tanzania's policy of nonalignment sometimes does appear to be an invitation to Communist penetration. It is a fact that Tanzania is host to more Communist diplomatic representation than any other African state. But in terms of political, economic, and cultural influence, the Western presence is paramount. The few hundred Chinese (the only sizable Communist contingent in the country) who are engaged in building a textile mill, a radio transmitter, and "surveying" a number of other development projects, are a less conspicuous force than the thousand-plus Western advisers, teachers, technicians, commercial representatives, and managers who stand athwart Tanzania's administrative and economic lifelines.

As for Zanzibar, it is true that in nearly three years of union with Tanganyika, the so-called Cuba of Africa has rarely submitted to direction from Dar es Salaam; but Zanzibar is also more remote from and less influential on the mainland than such capitalist-oriented neighbors as Kenya and Zambia. To the charge of communism, then, Nyerere has answered with characteristic humor; his tour was not a "long march" but a drive, and his youth movement is the Green Guard, not the red.

To the radical left in Nyerere's government and party, the Arusha Declaration came as a sign that their cause was in the ascendancy. Before their victory songs had faded, however, Nyerere once again displayed his mastery of pendulum politics. Having moved leftward at Arusha, he made a flanking gesture toward the right by assigning the important ministry of commerce and cooperatives to Paul Bomani, an effective administrator in whom local and foreign businessmen place considerable trust. Threading his way among those who seek to influence him. Nyerere maintained freedom of action to build a democratic Socialist state of his own design.

It is not, however, to the left that the Arusha Declaration is addressed. Rather it is to the nascent capitalist and bourgeois class of urban Africans that Nyerere has prescribed his own puritanical dedication to frugality and honesty in the public service. (Here he *has* borrowed from the Chinese.) Nyerere is determined that "black capitalism" shall not gain a foothold in Tanzania, and with good reason. Vulnerable to the attraction of partnerships in and directorships of foreign firms, Tanzanian leaders could all too easily yield to affluence—hence to foreign influence—and forget their obligation to the mass of the people who live at near-subsistence levels, far from the bright lights of the cities. Certainly this has happened in much of the rest of Africa, Nigeria having provided a recent and violent example of the consequences.

The seeds of capitalism and elitism had in fact already been planted in Tanzania. Some of them "flowered" in October 1966 when students at University College went on strike against the terms of national service. They were asked to give several months of their time for military training followed by twenty-one months in civilian jobs they would probably have entered anyway—but at half the customary salaries. Though they would still be earning many times the average per capita income of $60, and despite the fact that their education, the passkey to relative affluence, had been paid for by the Tanzanian government, the students protested. Nyerere sent more than three hundred of them home, or half the student body, to work on their fathers' *shambas* [patches of ground under cultivation] and learn a little humility.

Fear of Imported Values

As though to confirm his fear that imported values would nurture the growth of an African class system, Nyerere found that a number of African delegates to the November 1966 meeting of the Organization of African Unity had brought European advisers with them to Addis Ababa; some even carried credentials signed by expatriate officials in their own governments. In a fury, Nyerere denounced this bald display of "neocolonialism" and decried the "devils" at work in Africa who mocked its independence.

Hence the Arusha Declaration, which charts Tanzania's road to socialism, directs senior officials of the government, party, and trade unions to resist the siren call of quick wealth. It tells them to get rid of their shares and directorships in businesses, to stop the lucrative practice of using easily obtained loans to build houses for rental to foreign diplomats, advisers, and businessmen, and to draw only one salary. It will be recalled that Nyerere announced a . . . reduction in his own salary in October [1966], at the time of the student demonstrations, and pointedly said he assumed that other senior officials would glady do the same. They did, and high office in Tanzania can no longer be considered a horn of plenty. The Mercedes Benz sedan, formerly the status symbol par excellence, has become the stigma of the "exploiter."

Just what kind of socialism is this? There is nothing in the Arusha Declaration that the British Labour party, or most other Western European Socialist parties, could not support. Certainly the nationalization of a few banks and industries does not make "Socialist" a country 95 per cent of whose people are engaged in small-scale agriculture. Clearly, this is a "teaching." Nyerere, a former schoolmaster, is officially—and by preference—called *Mwalimu* (teacher), and his leadership is closer to that of the philosopher-king than any other in Africa, or for that matter the world. Whereas his socialism had previously been a state of mind prescribed in April 1962 under the rubric of *Ujamaa*—Swahili for "familyhood"—the Arusha Declaration proceeds from attitudes to action. Tanzanians are now called upon to act as well as think as Socialists. . . .

But what of the economic consequences of nationalizing the banks and industries? Managers of foreign banks, who were reasonably successful in adapting their institutions to the hazards of broken-field national planning after independence in 1961, and most economic advisers to the government, are frankly pessimistic about Tanzania's prospects under instant socialism. Whatever its merits—and few students of the underdeveloped world question the need for substantial government direction of and participation in the economy—socialism is far more difficult to construct in poor nations than in developed ones. For one thing, Tanzania lacks trained manpower to administer its complex new acquisitions. For another, there is nothing like nationalization to deter new investment and send capital scurrying from the country. (A lesson of economics is that exchange controls don't work.) Given the dearth of domestic capital and the timidity of its few local possessors, the socially alienated and politically vulnerable Indians, where will Tanzania find the resources to implement its development plan? The answer, and the second major theme of the Arusha Declaration, is self-reliance.

Response to Reality

The declaration says that it is "stupid" to rely on money as the major instrument of development because, first of all, "we shall not get the money," and secondly, external gifts and loans will "endanger our independence." But the doctrine of self-reliance is neither a retreat into economic isolationism nor a blueprint for autarchy. It is a realistic response to the exigencies of the present international economic order.

The gap between the rich nations and the poor continues to grow. Prices of the products of industrialized nations are rising; those of agricultural commodity producers are falling. Economic aid from the rich countries, generally cited at inflated levels owing to the high costs of tied procurement and the onerous terms of repayment, has by any measure been declining; often it barely covers the imminent costs of repayment of earlier loans. The dribble of private foreign investment, the vast bulk of which is directed to the oil and other mineral-producing countries, is often exceeded by the repatriation of profits. African industry, thwarted by its inability to compete in international markets, is typically left with those small-scale activities for which there is an adequate home market, e.g. the production of cigarettes and beer.

In sum, most of Africa faces bleak economic prospects despite the flow of aid and trade from the developed world. Such is the view of G. K. Helleiner, director of economic research at University College, Dar es Salaam. Tanzania, which at present relies principally on coffee, sisal, and cotton for export earnings, is particularly vulnerable because the prices of all three commodities are depressed and likely to remain so for some time to come.

But Nyerere's concept of self-reliance is also inspired by national pride. Tanzania has had the bitter experience of seeing proffered aid withdrawn because it pursued national policies not to the liking of the benefactors. Thus, when Nyerere agreed in 1964 to East German representation in Dar es Salaam at the consular level, West Germany invoked the now-fading Hallstein Doctrine and terminated most of its aid programs. And when Nyerere became the first to carry out the 1965 Organization of African Unity resolution to break diplomatic relations with Britain if it did not take determined steps to end the Rhodesian rebellion, Tanzania lost a virtually certain British loan of £7 million—almost $20 million —money which had already been allocated and, in effect, spent by Tanzanian ministries. Even United States assistance dwindled for a time in 1965 owing to a pair of unfortunate diplomatic contretemps. . . .

Communist economic assistance has been equally troublesome and no more productive. The negotiation of a proffered Soviet loan fell through in 1965 over the terms of its use and repayment. And while Chinese aid has ostensibly been free of political strings, the commodity exchange agreements which govern it have proved costly and of questionable value to Tanzania. Thus, Tanzania's experiences with foreign economic aid, as well as with trade, have brought a loss of confidence and fostered skepticism of its utility.

What Is To Be Done?

Is Tanzania's economic retrenchment, then, a retreat into economic primitivism? Not if one considers that self-reliance may bring a country to grips with its own problems, rather than the real or imagined problems heretofore blamed on imperialism, capitalism, neocolonialism, and even communism. President Nyerere, having translated *Julius Caesar* into Swahili, apparently believes that "the fault, dear Brutus, is not in our stars. . . ." He calls for more work, increased production, and a greater sense of self-sacrifice. "We have been oppressed a great deal," says the Arusha Declaration, "we have been exploited a great deal, and we have been disregarded a great deal. It is our weakness that has led to our being oppressed, exploited, and disregarded."

In Western terms, the belt-tightening to come is a striking form of self-help based on the assumption that only through their own efforts can African countries develop economically and retain their sovereign integrity. It is not, however, a renunciation of foreign trade and aid, without which Tanzania's produce would rot in the tropical sun and its growing public sector would surely crumble. But self-reliance does place the burden of economic development— as nationalization places control of the major means of production —in Tanzanian hands.

Chou En-lai said in 1964 that the "prospects for revolution in Africa are excellent." In their haste to decry this implicit threat to their regimes, a good many African leaders overlooked the fact that the continent was already on the fringes of revolution—a revolution fueled by the decreasing ability of governments to create the opportunities their people demand. To a large extent, that is what the military coups and the entrenchment of authoritarian rule are all about. Though it is invoked too freely and too often, the phrase "revolution of rising expectations" describes what is happening in much of Africa, if not today, then surely tomorrow.

At Arusha, Tanzania's leaders charted a course for carrying forward their own revolution gradually and peacefully. The economic and political risks are very high, and Nyerere understands the hazards he faces. But the alternative of violent revolution is far more hazardous, as the rest of the Third World is learning and as Africa, too, may come to know.

KENYA'S ECONOMY: A PROFILE [3]

Capital: Nairobi

Population: 9.4 million

Area: 225,000 square miles (somewhat smaller than Texas)

Principal Exports (1964): coffee (33 per cent), sisal (13 per cent), tea (13 per cent), pyrethrum (5 per cent)

U.S. AID Investment Guarantees: convertibility, expropriation, war or civil disturbances, extended risk

Kenya consists essentially of three regions. In the southwest, gently undulating plateau lands are broken by the north-south Rift Valley, marked by a string of lakes. In the central area, snow-capped peaks of extinct volcanoes (Mt. Kenya: seventeen thousand feet) rise before the land slowly dips in the east towards the coastal plain fringing the Indian Ocean.

Kenya contains some of the best agricultural land in East Africa, although more than half of the country is arid, with little potential for irrigation. Agricultural production is centered in the more humid south—on the cool plateau, in the Lake Victoria basin, and along the tropical coast. The southwestern region contains most of the population, which is 97 per cent African. Asians (183,000) — as well as Arabs (36,000)—are generally involved in trading activities. Europeans (49,000), who at first were mostly farmers and administrators, have in recent years turned to commerce and industry in the urban centers.

[3] From *East and Central Africa—A Survey of Six Developing Countries.* Foreign Information Service. First National City Bank. New York. '66. p 6-9. Reprinted by permission.

Structure of the Economy

Kenya's economy is based primarily on agriculture and live-stock raising, which account for approximately 40 per cent of gross domestic product [GDP] and earn 80 per cent of the country's foreign exchange. GDP was estimated at $778 million for 1964, a 7 per cent increase over 1963 at current prices, or about a 4 per cent increase in real terms. The rate of growth was dampened in 1965 by a drought which cut farm incomes. Per capita GDP amounted to $83 in 1964.

Although Kenya is the world's largest exporter of pyrethrum (used in insecticides), its main export is coffee, which is expected to maintain its position despite the limitation set on future plantings by the International Coffee Agreement. Other exports are sisal and tea—for which expansion prospects are brighter—meat and meat preparations, and hides and skins. Tourism has grown in recent years, and today earns half as much foreign exchange as does coffee.

A recent decline in livestock raising and crop production has been attributed to fragmentation of land holdings arising from a resettlement scheme designed to transfer two million European-owned acres to forty thousand African farmers. Output is expected to rebound when the land transfer is completed.

No mineral resources of consequence have yet been uncovered by a geological survey scheduled for completion in 1966. The only significant production is of soda ash, which has suffered a recent decline. The country is equally deficient in fuels, including wood. Domestic electricity production is based on imported fuels, and must be supplemented by supplies originating in Uganda and Tanzania. This arrangement should be adequate to satisfy electricity demand over the next few years, but plans are under way to develop hydroelectric power resources to augment domestic generating capacity.

Long distance transport between major centers and the Indian Ocean port of Mombasa is provided by the railway which crosses into Uganda. However, improved roads are needed to serve agricultural areas.

Kenya, despite the lack of fuel resources, has become the most important manufacturing and business center in East Africa. Manufacturing industry, which now accounts for 10 per cent of GDP, has developed around the major cities, with a concentration in the Nairobi area. Initially, industry was based on the processing of agricultural commodities for export, but recently plants producing consumer goods have experienced rapid expansion. A variety of new projects have either been completed or are planned, notably an oil refinery at Mombasa, a fertilizer factory (which would make Kenya self-sufficient in fertilizers), a synthetic-textile plant, and a plastics factory.

Foreign Trade and Payments

Kenya normally runs an external trade deficit partially offset by an export surplus with its partners in the East African Common Market, Uganda and Tanzania.

In recent years, tea, sisal, and coffee exports have increased in both quantity and value, while pyrethrum is experiencing a slight dip. Meat and dairy products, after a sharp rise in the early 1960's (when they tripled in value), are currently on the decline.

Even though the United Kingdom is still Kenya's major trading partner, accounting for about a third of total exports and imports, exchanges with other countries are increasing. The EEC [European Economic Community] countries, particularly West Germany, have gained in importance, and U.S. trade growth looks promising. Although the American share of Kenya's total trade normally amounts to no more than 7-9 per cent, U.S. exports stepped up from $13.5 million in 1964 to an estimated $24 million . . . [in 1965].

The main source of foreign financial assistance remains the United Kingdom, which provided $50 million in grants and loans during the fiscal year ended March 1965, slightly more than in the previous year. In addition, United States AID [Agency for International Development] and other American agencies have extended more than $35 million in grants and loans to Kenya since 1948. Total United States economic and technical aid amounted to $6.4 million in 1964.

Economic Policies and Planning

After completing a series of development plans, Kenya embarked in 1964 upon a six-year development plan calling for a

6 per cent average annual increase in GDP (measured in current prices), coupled with a virtual doubling of exports and a 70 per cent rise in agricultural incomes. The plan entails an investment of about $900 million; it is hoped that more than half of this total will be provided by private investors. Under the Foreign Investment Protection Bill passed in 1964, various legal guarantees are extended to foreign investors.

Government assistance to the private sector takes several forms. Small African-owned industry is aided by loans from the Industrial and Commercial Development Corporation. New industrial projects are encouraged by the Development Finance Company of Kenya through equity participation.

KENYA'S ECONOMIC PRAGMATISM [4]

"The typical American businessman used to come here on safari and leave," says a banker in Kenya's capital city of Nairobi. "Now, a lot of them who come here as tourists get interested in business prospects and start looking around."

Nairobi is still a starting-out place for safaris—and the white hunter in bush jacket can still be seen striding through the New Stanley Hotel. But this sparkling city of 350,000 people is becoming known for bigger game than the wildlife in the surrounding East African bush—and the new trophies are business enterprises. This is because Kenya, a land noted for blood oaths and settler slaughters fifteen years ago, is today one of Africa's most stable countries and a magnet for such U.S. companies as Union Carbide, Colgate-Palmolive, and Ward Foods.

The change in both mood and substance is due largely to the policies of Kenya President Jomo Kenyatta. Jailed by the British during the 1950's—when Kenya was still a British colony—as the alleged organizer of the Mau Mau, Kenyatta has emerged as a national hero. Above all, he has been remarkably successful in persuading his countrymen to set aside their tribal and racial differences and to work for national unity.

    [4] Article, "Business Makes a Kenya Safari." *Business Week.* p 108+. S. 2, '67. Reprinted from the September 2, 1967, issue of *Business Week* by special permission. Copyrighted © 1967 by McGraw-Hill, Inc.

An important part of that unity effort has required the retention of some once-hated Western influence. Today, nearly four years after it achieved independence, Kenya still has 1,700 Britons in its civil service, and some of them hold important jobs. But what is perhaps far more significant is that Western businessmen operate in Kenya without fear of nationalization—in sharp contrast to nearby Tanzania, which earlier this year nationalized foreign-owned banks and some foreign-owned companies. [See first two articles in this section.]

Kenyatta's moderate policies bring criticism from the more nationalistic Africans, but it is criticism that does not take into account Kenyatta's record on the farm. Kenyatta points out that many European farmers have already been pushed out of Kenya and that since 1961, 1.2 million acres of Kenya's farmland has been turned over to Africans.

Payoff

Kenyatta's overriding concern with what is pragmatic—as opposed to what is ideological—seems to be paying off in the economic sphere. He has drawn up an economic-development plan that stresses both public and private enterprise, and which sets a growth goal of 6.3 per cent a year through 1970. But the goal appears to be on the conservative side; last year, Kenya's gross domestic product grew at an 8 per cent rate. Manufacturing increased smartly, at a 9 per cent clip, but the principal credit goes to good crops—agriculture is still the mainstay of the economy.

To maintain this growth record, Kenyatta is counting on plenty of help from the outside—both in aid (which comes largely from Britain) and in foreign investment. But his liberal investment program is designed to bring in businessmen from everywhere—not just Britain.

The program is beginning to show results. Kenya has for some time been looked on as a British preserve by many U.S. businessmen, but there are now nearly seventy U.S. companies with offices or plants there. In 1962, there were only twenty. U.S. investment in Kenya—many of the U.S. companies have set up shop just in the past two or three years—is growing rapidly and now probably exceeds $100 million. Still, foreign investment is largely a story of the one-time colonizer—British companies still control about 80 per cent of it; U.S. interests, 15 per cent.

The center of Kenya's economic activity is of course Nairobi, and the center of Nairobi's economic activity is Government Road, the home of handsome new office buildings, where African workers in Western dress mingle with European and American business-men. Another notable thoroughfare is flower-lined Uhuru (Free-dom) Road (formerly Queen Elizabeth Highway), down which cars and trucks travel to the seaside city of Mombasa—sometimes at a rate that causes rush-hour traffic jams. Finally, Nairobi's out-skirts are sprinkled with new plants busily processing food, making textiles and other light-industry products.

The British built up Nairobi to be a center of East African finance, trade, and transportation—and succeeded. But until about fifteen years ago, the pace was sufficiently pastoral that lions some-times wandered onto the runway at Nairobi airport. Today, the roaring is done by jet airplanes, which make fifty flights in and out of Nairobi every week.

More and more U.S. businessmen are on those flights, and they are thinking about other things than safaris.

Union Carbide Corporation, in partnership with a Kenya gov-ernment corporation, is about to complete a $1.8 million plant at Nakuru that will make seventy million batteries a year (many of which will go into transistor radios, the latest Kenya status sym-bol). Colgate-Palmolive Company is making detergents (Fab), cleansers (Ajax), and toothpaste in a $1 million plant it opened at Nairobi in late 1965. Another member of the Nairobi business community is Pfizer International, which produces pesticides at a small plant there. Other U.S. companies in Kenya include Phillips Petroleum Company, with an interest in a plastic-chair producer at Mombasa; Caltex and Esso, which own two-thirds of an oil refinery, also at Mombasa; Crown Cork & Seal Corporation, which is making bottle caps; and Eastman Kodak, distributing and pro-cessing film.

Potential

This processing and manufacturing activity in Kenya seems likely to grow. For one thing, it seems to be profitable—at least for some companies. ("A 10 per cent return on investment is about right here," says one U.S. manufacturer.) Another reason is that last June the Kenya government signed a Treaty of East African Cooperation with its neighbors, Tanzania and Uganda. The treaty provides for the continuance of East-African common services (airlines, railroads, etc.) set up by the British in colonial days, but its main significance for businessmen is that the three countries won't restrict each other's imports. Thus, instead of being limited to Kenya's nine million potential customers, businessmen have a three-nation market of about twenty-eight million.

Says William A. Moore, Eastern Africa general sales manager for Union Carbide: "The treaty is very important to us. With Japanese interests going into Tanzania, and Swiss into Uganda, it gives us guaranteed access for our products."

Signing of the treaty may also bring action by several U.S. rubber companies, which have been thinking of setting up tire plants in Kenya. Also, it probably will encourage more companies to move sales offices to Nairobi from such cities as Rome and Beirut, once widely used as bases for serving East Africa.

Another area of business that is beginning to attract U.S. interest in Kenya is agriculture and food processing. With the assistance of American aid (about $10 million a year) and Kenya government support, various schemes are being worked on to get U.S. food companies interested.

One of them is Del Monte Corporation, already helping Kenyans can pineapples and vegetables for shipment to Europe. It reportedly now is spearheading a group that may go into cattle-feeding and processing on a substantial scale, with the meat to be shipped to European markets. Ward Foods International has been shipping beef out of East Africa for some months, and is now working on a complex project in Kenya to raise cattle, and market the meat abroad. Total cost of the deal could come to $18 million.

Because of its climate—cool by African standards—and its wealth of wild animals, Kenya has always been a magnet to Europeans. Now, with the help of jet-airplane service, tourism is beginning to take off; last year, 106,320 persons visited the country, a 31 per cent increase over 1965. U.S. companies are moving to take advantage of it: Inter-Continental Hotels and Trans World Airlines, Inc. are investing in new hotels in Nairobi. Pan American World Airways operates New York-Nairobi service.

Most safaris nowadays are "camera" safaris rather than "shooting" safaris—they are considerably cheaper, for one thing (a big Hemingway-type hunting safari can cost $8,000 to $10,000). An American-owned company in Kenya, Safari Air Services, Ltd., does about 30 per cent to 40 per cent of its one-million-dollar-a-year business running charter flights for tourists and businessmen, and is now working on a two-day "safari-of-the-week" for Nairobi businessmen who have weekends free.

This seemingly idyllic country, of course, isn't without its problems. And some of them have a direct effect on business.

For one thing, the pressure to "Africanize" business and government is growing more intense—as it is in most African countries. A survey recently showed that only about 7 per cent of executive and supervisory jobs in Kenya were held by Africans. Kenyatta understandably wants this figure to grow. But the process of training them is difficult and expensive. And the demands on the business community for still more Africanization will grow.

Then too, conflicts between Africans and Asians living in Kenya are sharpening. Those who notice it most are the country's 200,000 Indians, who have a near-monopoly over small business. The Kenyans feel the Indians, who operate family-owned businesses for the most part, are deliberately seeking to keep them out. The pressures have been felt. Some Indian Sikhs, who held skilled jobs in the construction trades, have left the country. [For further details on this problem, see Section IV, below.]

Future

By far the most crucial question, though, is what will happen when Kenyatta—now in his seventies—is gone. Kenyatta's prestige is so high that he has effectively kept tribalism submerged in the general striving for national unity. But his successor may not be equally adroit at avoiding conflicts between Kikuyus and Luos, the two main tribes. Also, there could be a renewed push by such leftists as Oginga Odinga, who has been accused of accepting big sums from Communist countries. "Double-O," as Odinga is called, was dumped by Kenyatta as vice president last year, but he still has some popularity and a comeback in the future can't be ruled out. (Paradoxically, Odinga was one of Kenya's most successful native businessmen; he operated a trucking and transport company.)

In the event Kenyatta dies, his successor will be named by parliament to serve until the next national election in 1970. Strong possibilities to succeed him include Tom Mboya, Kenya's brilliant economic planner, and Daniel Arap Moi, a vice president who has lately been gaining increasing political support. Both of these men probably would continue Kenyatta's policies.

UGANDA'S ECONOMY: A PROFILE [5]

Capital: Kampala

Population: 7.5 million

Area: 94,000 square miles (somewhat smaller than Oregon)

Principal Exports (1964): coffee (55 per cent), cotton (25 per cent)

U.S. AID Investment Guarantees: convertibility, expropriation, war or civil disturbances, extended risk

A landlocked country, Uganda lies in the upper basin of the Nile, and consists mostly of a plateau four thousand feet high with scattered mountains rising to almost seventeen thousand feet. This elevation is responsible for a temperate climate despite the proximity to the Equator. Rainfall is generally ample, and fairly well distributed; however, a dry zone stretches across the country from northeast to southwest.

The population is concentrated in the south, particularly along the Lake Victoria shore, where most plantations, commerce, and

[5] From *East and Central Africa—A Survey of Six Developing Countries*. Foreign Information Service. First National City Bank. New York. '66. p 9-11. Reprinted by permission.

industry are located. Uganda is traditionally rural, although towns have been expanding in recent years as the result of a growing influx of workers. Typically, Africans (99 per cent of population) are engaged in farming, Asians (76,000) in trading, and Europeans (11,000) in professional and technical work.

Structure of the Economy

Uganda has a predominantly farm economy, and agriculture occupies 90 per cent of its population. GDP [gross domestic product], after a slump in 1961 and 1962, grew to $543 million in 1964, a 10 per cent increase at current prices over the previous year. Per capita GDP amounted to $72 in 1964.

Subsistence agriculture and tending of livestock account for the bulk of farm activity. Only 25 per cent of the arable land is used for cash crops, and even less (86,000 acres) is allotted to plantation cultivation. Originally, the main export crop was cotton, which reached a peak in 1936-1937. Since then it has declined in value, and has been overtaken in recent years by coffee, of which Uganda is the largest producer in the Commonwealth. Other cash crops include tea, sugar, and tobacco; the latter two commodities are mostly consumed within East Africa.

Mineral resources are of minor importance, and consist mainly of copper. There are some deposits of phosphates, tin, tungsten, beryl, and others, but copper production amounts to about 87 per cent of total mineral output. Copper reserves are expected to be exhausted within a decade unless the exploration for new deposits currently under way proves productive.

There are no fuel resources other than wood. About three fifths of the forest land is preserved to prevent soil erosion and retain the water supply. Hydroelectric power is Uganda's greatest asset. The Owen Falls hydroelectric station on the Nile, which has an ultimate capacity of 150,000 kilowatts, is the largest in East Africa. Plans for other hydroelectric schemes are being drawn up or carried out.

The development of Uganda's economy began with the construction of a nine-hundred-mile-long railway to the port of Mombasa in Kenya. The necessary link was made when the railroad reached the eastern shore of Lake Victoria in 1901. This outlet to the sea is supplemented by an excellent domestic feeder road system, and by water transport.

Existing industries include a small steel mill, a meat packing plant, a distillery, and factories producing fertilizer, cement, corrugated sheet iron, sugar, and textiles. Pharmaceutical and paper-making plants and a glass factory are among the facilities being developed. However, expansion is hampered by shortages of raw materials and of skilled labor.

Foreign Trade and Payments

Uganda usually runs a sizable external trade surplus. The favorable balance of trade reached a record level in 1964, when exports were double the import total, but the export surplus was cut down in 1965 by a dip in export earnings.

In recent years, low export prices have adversely affected income from cotton sales, while earnings from copper, tea, and—until last year [1965]—from coffee have increased considerably. Tourism, though still a minor item, has shown a rapid rate of growth; in 1964 it earned $5.6 million, twice as much as in 1963.

The United Kingdom traditionally is Uganda's major partner, accounting for just under 20 per cent of its total trade (exports plus imports). About a third of Uganda's imports is supplied by the United Kingdom, and Japan and Germany together account for another third. The United States is Uganda's major customer, taking about 25 per cent of its exports since 1962, and is now rivaling Britain in its share of Uganda's total trade. Uganda's raw cotton is marketed mainly in India and West Germany, and coffee in the United States and Britain.

British economic aid to Uganda totaled $11.8 million in fiscal 1964-1965, compared with $15.7 million the year before. Assistance is also being provided by the United States AID, the World Bank, Germany, mainland China, Yugoslavia, and Russia.

Economic Policies and Planning

Following an IBRD [International Bank for Reconstruction and Development] study, a five-year plan was drawn up for the period 1961-1966. Revised upwards in 1963, it calls for a $308 million investment, of which the government would contribute more than half; an annual increase of 5 per cent in national income is projected. By May 1965, less than half of this planned investment had been realized because of a lack of foreign capital and trained personnel. A second five-year development plan, 1966-1971, calling for an expenditure of $644 million, has been drawn up; it envisages growth not only in agriculture but also in the industrial sector of the economy.

A major factor in the promoting of these plans is the government-owned Uganda Development Corporation, which seeks to develop new enterprises in partnership with private firms. It is currently engaged in copper production, in manufacture of piece goods, cement, metal and enamel ware, in the mining and hotel industries, and in agriculture—especially tea raising. The Foreign Investment (Protection) Act and the Uganda Industrial Charter outline the incentives offered domestic and foreign capital, and the investor's rights concerning repatriation of profits and capital.

UGANDA'S SLOW BUT STEADY PROGRESS [6]

Slow but sure progress is being made by this East African republic toward development of diversified agriculture.

A development slowdown last year [1967] after a . . . [period] of exceptionally rapid growth was caused by lower output and lower prices for coffee and cotton, the country's main cash crops. Exports of these crops earn more than three fourths of Uganda's foreign exchange.

Much of Uganda's high development rate from 1963 to 1966 was the result of an export boom in coffee, cotton and copper, and the investment of accumulated reserves.

[6] From "Uganda Gain Slow But Sure." New York *Times.* p 60. Ja. 26, '68. Copyright © 1968 by The New York Times Company. Reprinted by permission.

In July 1966, the country's second five-year plan was started with emphasis on diversification and expansion of both cash and food crops to decrease overdependence on coffee and cotton. The plan stresses financing from internal sources of more than two thirds of the $644 million of projected development expenditures.

It was envisioned that the balance of plan financing would come from external private investment and international aid sources. Because of the soundness of the drafting and management of the plan so far, this expectation shows considerable promise of being fulfilled.

Rein on Credit

A tight rein has been applied to credit and to recurrent government expenditures. Import controls have been increased to give priority on foreign exchange to capital equipment and materials needed for the development plan. A costly subsidy to cotton growers has been eliminated.

Increased taxes have produced revenue somewhat higher than anticipated, but the government has shown a determination to hold down regular expenses and transfer surpluses to the development budget. In the current fiscal year, it is expected that $21 million will be transferred from the recurrent to the development budget and some surplus should still be left for the building up of reserves.

Despite the lower returns on coffee and cocoa, the over-all rate of Uganda's economic growth has continued at a satisfactory level. There has been a decrease in the relatively small, but important, production of copper, the country's chief mineral export. But in construction and manufacturing, new development and investment have continued at a high level.

Extensive programs for the expansion of tea to make it a major export have been started. Sugar is expected to provide a growing surplus for export and large expansion of tobacco exports is expected....

Potentially, the most significant development for Uganda last year was her partnership in a new agreement for East African cooperation with the neighboring countries of Kenya and Tanzania. The agreement should greatly increase the possibilities for new industrial development in Uganda as well as her exports to East African markets.

Under the agreement, Uganda will be able to restrict imports from more industrially developed Kenya, while gaining duty-free access to the Kenyan market. While this benefit will be for a limited time, up to eight years in the case of any restricted article, it should give Uganda opportunities to catch up with Kenya industrially.

IV. RACE AND SOCIETY

EDITOR'S INTRODUCTION

What intrigues Americans most about Africa in general and East Africa in particular? It can hardly be the area's economic problems or political developments, though at times these—particularly the latter—have a storybook quality. In fact, it is the charm and beauty of East Africa and its people that most enthrall us—the wild animals, the primitive tribes, the strange customs, the natural beauty of the landscape. East Africa is not only a paradise for the zoologist and the botanist; it is a paradise for the sociologist and ethnologist, too. With their diverse races, tribes, and languages Kenya, Tanzania, and Uganda offer a wealth of sociological material for study.

The five articles in this section explore some of the salient cultural and social problems facing this part of the world. What role do women play in East African society? What are the popular attitudes toward education? In an era of modernization, how are the primitive tribes faring? And what of racial problems since independence—do whites, Indians, and blacks live together now in peace and equality?

In the first selection a correspondent for the New York *Times* describes some marriage customs in Kenya and in so doing casts revealing light on the role of women in East Africa, generally. Next a Kenyan educator argues for the need to develop "an academic spirit" among East African youth as a basis for educational progress. In the third article a curator at the American Museum of Natural History describes the desperate plight of the primitive Ik tribe in Uganda. The last two articles deal with the fate of East Africa's whites and Indians in the years since independence.

THE ROLE OF WOMEN IN EAST AFRICA [1]

Women are different now [said Chief Njiri Karanja, leaning forward on his stool to pull one stiff, sinewy leg over the other]. Women are getting clever. They are wearing expensive dresses instead of skins. They are painting their faces with cosmetics instead of mud. They are wearing high wigs that look like beehives. All these things cost money, and women didn't know about money before. Now there are school fees, too; it is very expensive to educate many children.

Let me tell you: I had fifty-two wives, and finally they were like fifty-two pots of poison. If I had to start over now, I think one at a time would be plenty.

This ancient Kikuyu chief is more than just a quaint relic of Kenya's ancient past. He symbolizes not only the old values and customs—of marriage, of family and of social stability—but the new problems brought about by money, industrialization, urbanization and the other twentieth-century attributes which Africa has become heir to. In his time he has seen the old ways in frontal attack from the new, has watched them bend and blend, and has known some of them to buckle entirely.

In the old days, under the old customs, Chief Njiri was a man of power. He was rich, as the Kikuyu reckoned wealth, and could afford many wives. Because of the competition to marry his daughters, he could demand as many as fifteen cattle in bride-price instead of the usual five or six, some of which he added to his herds and some he set aside to acquire more wives.

As long as land was plentiful each wife got her own *shamba,* her patch of ground on which to grow the corn and beans she needed to support herself and the children she brought into the world. To Chief Njiri each wife, apart from being a fresh and lively new soul-mate, was another pair of hands. Finally, he had his women hoeing acres of corn up and down most of the hillsides around Kinona, north of Nairobi. His big herds of cattle wandered over the uncultivated slopes and his sons were spread as far as Kijabe, in the Rift Valley.

[1] From "Kenya Report: Market in Brides," by Lawrence Fellows, staff correspondent. New York *Times Magazine.* p 12+. F. 19, '67. Copyright © 1967 by The New York Times Company. Reprinted by permission.

In the old days Chief Njiri had to guard against being plundered by the Masai or some other neighboring tribe looking for cattle, women and other valuable items of booty. The bigger his family and the bigger and stronger the tribe, the less likely was that sort of disaster. In addition, infant mortality and famine made family-building a matter of survival.

Each new bride brought interlocking and unending responsibilities to new clans within the tribe, and this helped give cohesion to the tribe. Polygamy and the practice of marrying the girls off as soon as they were nubile insured that the most was got out of a woman's fecundity, and helped secure the future for the tribe.

A Woman's Virtues

In such a system, the place of the woman was special, but quite low. The virtues she was supposed to bother about were discipline, childbearing and the unity of the family and clan. It worked out well for the family and the clan, and also for the man. But not so much for the woman, who was pretty much of a chattel.

Even today the women retain much of this old position. Few have broken through the old barriers to an education and a career. Any day on the paths around Nairobi the evidence is there to see: a man, if he can bring himself to carry anything, will be swinging a little stick, while his wife staggers on behind, bent almost horizontal under a heavy load of firewood held from her forehead by a leather strap that wrinkles her shaven head and heightens her earnest and unhappy look. At home she wields the hoe; he sits in the shade and drinks *pombe,* the thick brew she made from the corn she grew and harvested.

In Uganda the more prominent Bahima men are still in a position to insist that their brides be fattened on milk, and the Bahima women are some of the most statuesque and beautifully built women on the continent. They have to be forcibly fed, and are beaten and stuffed so full that sometimes they cannot stand up alone and have to creep through the wedding ceremony on all fours, or be pushed through it by a gang of old women in attendance.

In the kingdom of Ankole in Uganda the keepers of the morals no longer lightly throw wayward girls into the Kagera River. Yet when a well-behaved girl is married, she is expected to provide sexual entertainment for all her husband's brothers as well. The same goes for the Masai in Kenya, although the service is extended to any visitor from the tribe, provided he is in the right age group. If the Masai visitor puts the woman in a family way, her husband is flattered; to him it is a matter of building his social security.

Yet, under the traditional system, no woman in Africa should ever find herself destitute. None should be turned into a nervous wreck, none should feel her life is unfulfilled. Even if she should somehow feel discontented, under the comfortably old shelter of custom, there was no expectation that she would be left unmarried.

Moreover, in some corners of Tanzania there is still polyandry, where the women take on as many husbands as they can afford, or think they have time for. . . . And among the Langi in Uganda a woman may divorce her husband for impotence, nonmaintenance, cruelty, practicing witchcraft, quarrelsomeness, incompatibility, assault, laziness or foolishness. While some may wonder that there are any Langi women at all who stand by their husbands, it is true in most African societies, even where a woman cannot divorce her husband, she can leave him if he is too cruel to her or if he refuses to eat the food she puts before him.

The Cost of Brides

Bride-price, whether by the Zulu name of *lobola* or the Kikuyu label of *ruracio,* was another of the old steady customs with which the social fabric was knit. The idea of placing a monetary value on a woman is deeply imbedded in many societies around the world, but bride-price in Africa was more than just that. It had some of the flavor of playing cards for money: the game was still the prime consideration, but playing even for pennies tended to spice the hand and make it a less trivial undertaking.

It was, first, the way the suitor paid compensation to his bride's parents for all they had spent on her from the time she was born. Before cash crept into it, the price might have been in cattle, sheep, goats, copper ingots, gold, beads, spears or anything valuable, and would have covered even the calabashes she broke and the honey she spilled as a child. It was an earnest of the suitor's good faith, for not only was it expensive but it meant he would have his bride's clan around his neck for the rest of his life. And it was a way of stabilizing the marriage, because if the bride ran home on her wedding night the father would have to hand back the whole lot. (Or more likely, he would give his daughter a good thrashing and send her back to her new husband.)

But the old days of close tribal cohesion and huge, interlocked families are going. Disease is being controlled, famine is being relieved, tribal wars are being discouraged, the arguments for polygamy are therefore weaker—and the women are beginning to feel the time has come for a change. Peace among wives in some of the larger households is becoming more and more difficult to maintain. The letters columns in newspapers from one side of the continent to the other are loaded with complaints that demonstrate how fiercely the women resent both polygamy and the unmistakable air of purchase that seems to be settling around bride-price.

In some places the women are gradually getting their way.

In Rwanda, the Ivory Coast and elsewhere in Africa where the pressures from the Catholic Church and from organized groups of women have been too strong to resist, polygamy has been abolished by law: yet these governments know it will be years before their people will pay full attention to the new laws.

In Ethiopia, where polygamy is forbidden by law to all but Moslems, the Ethiopians have a traditional form of marriage called *Be Damoz*, a fairly casual arrangement fixed usually on a monthly basis with a salary for the woman. The children from these marriages are considered legitimate, but the woman has no real claim on her husband's estate apart from whatever salary there might be in arrears. The courts are beginning to treat these women more generously, especially those who entered into marriage as virgins.

Impact of Urbanization

Urbanization and the evolution of a money economy are having a much faster effect on the old customs than the whole chorus of angry female voices. The need for money has been made inevitable by the desire for education and by the growing demand for bicycles, radios, suits, motor scooters and all the other accouterments of "civilization."

Even a skilled and relatively well-paid worker in Nairobi, earning as much as $150 a month, will have to weigh his resources carefully before he thinks seriously about taking on a second wife, especially if her family is going to find out how much he is earning. The new importance of money is shaking the ground under polygamy, bride-price and the whole lot of customs around marriage and the family.

More often than not, however, bride-price is accepted by educated Africans as a worth-while institution. A lot of young people would like to see bride-price retained, but brought back down to reasonable proportions, so that the traditions of family solidarity can be preserved without sending newlyweds deep into debt. It need not be regarded as any more commercial than the presentation of an engagement ring.

The Africans who argue for the retention of bride-price like to talk about the awful examples of inexpensive marriage and easy divorce in the United States. They liken taking a wife there to checking a book out of the public library: you can have it if you are attracted by the cover, and return it if you tire of it after the first couple of chapters. The Africans pay for their books and brides, and think carefully before they decide which ones they want to keep. It is just that the prices, at least of brides, are increasing so rapidly.

With bride-prices rising, payment on the installment plan has become almost universally accepted in Africa. It was always that way among the Karamojong in Uganda. The difference there was that the marriage was not considered binding until the whole bride-price had been paid. As this could take up to fifteen years, it was sometimes hard on the woman who happened to marry a slow-moving husband.

Generally, however, there are said to be few defaulters on wife-buying installment plans. Men who fall behind in their payments are hauled before tribal elders who examine their means and lay out schedules for future payment. The elders have no legal standing in most places in Africa, but to disobey them means to cut loose permanently from the clan.

Strong Clan Ties Remain

And the ties to the clan, even in the new Africa, are still strong —but, in the new Africa, they create their own special problems. For obligations of hospitality apply to clan members wherever they go, and when they move off the land into the cities this can make their lives very complicated indeed.

A family with a house in town is almost never without house guests, some of whom can be expected never to leave. Any African home is a reception center for all clan members. In the village a visiting relative might bring a chicken and, if it is a woman, help with the work and the children. But in the city the visitors more often sit and mope and, if they are waiting for paying jobs, sit and mope for a long, long time. Among the Bantu tribes, the parents are the worst hazard; they can come when they are hard up and take whatever they want out of the house.

One young family man in Salisbury [Rhodesia] where overcrowding in African homes is strictly against the law, simply slips out of his home when it gets too crowded and calls the police. He acts as surprised and unhappy as all the others when the premises are cleared by the long arm of the law, but he is laughing inside; he will not be blamed and he knows it will be at least a week before the relatives begin piling up in his home again.

Yet the same man takes advantage of the system when he heads on vacation trips to visit his second wife in a village deep in the bush. He takes a bus for about half the distance. It costs him only half as much that way, and from where he gets off the bus he can make his way from clan member to clan member, by a slightly circuitous route, to his second home at no additional cost.

This man's approach to the clan responsibilities he acquired with each of his wives may be a twisted one, but he is keeping his own two immediate families together on a single salary, and send-

ing his two batches of sons to school. If he were to treat his two sets
of in-laws as custom requires, he would soon have nothing. He
has long since cast out any thought of acquiring a third wife and
a third network of expense and responsibility. Like Chief Njiri in
Kinona, he appreciates that the custom has been overtaken by the
times.

DEVELOPING THE ACADEMIC SPIRIT IN EAST AFRICA [2]

The three East African nations—Kenya, Uganda, and Tanzania
—like most other developing nations of the world that have recently become independent, are engaged in combating human
problems of immense magnitude and complexity. The problems
themselves are basic: to be able to produce enough food in the
right combination to feed our populations so that not only will
their bellies be filled, but their bodies will be well and truly nour-
ished; to be able to combat disease not only by curative methods
but, much more importantly, by preventive means; to be able to
open the eyes of our people to what is going on around them
through education of the right type. This education has to take
into account what is going on in the world at large, for the world
has become, at least spatially, one. Our models can no longer be
drawn only from our immediate environment.

The problems, however, become much more complex when
their over-all setting is taken into consideration, as it must be if
any lasting solution is to be achieved. For instance, the problems
involved in the production of food are no longer those of one per-
son producing enough food for himself and his family, but of individuals producing that amount and enough more to feed the
thousands of town dwellers who themselves are not in a position
to produce any at all. Add to this the problem of general increase
in population, and the fact that, as part of this, the traditional
methods of agriculture are no longer efficacious; take into account

[2] Article in *Bulletin of the Atomic Scientists*. 22:19-21. O. '66. "Developing the
Academic Spirit in East Africa," by David P. S. Wasawo is reprinted with permission from the October 1966 issue of the *Bulletin of the Atomic Scientists*. Copyright
1966 by the Educational Foundation for Nuclear Science. The author is deputy principal
of University College, University of East Africa, Nairobi, Kenya.

the general level of education in modern agricultural methods and the traditional human conservatism in plant and animal husbandry; then one begins to appreciate the immensity and complexity of the problems with which our governments are faced in the field of food production.

The complexity of our health problems is also heightened by our recent history. The problems of epidemiology in villages with scattered homesteads and limited communications are, in large measure, quite different from those of towns with concentrated populations, and with efficient communications such as road, sea, and air transportation. Furthermore, whole populations have been exposed to new diseases against which they had hardly developed any natural resistance, let alone had any traditional know-how in combating them. Our new human relationships imply the need for a fresh outlook on preventive measures to be taken in relation to disease, and all these presuppose new thinking and new efforts to be made.

The Ends of Education

I give these two examples in the areas of food and health in order to throw more clearly into relief the problem of appropriate areas of academic preoccupation. It may be said, and it has been said in some influential quarters, that East Africa is so preoccupied with these basic problems that it would be a luxury to pursue knowledge just for its own sake, to be "purely academic," as the traditional definition goes. What East Africa needs, we are told, is the definition of our economic and social objectives, followed by a research effort to realize these objectives—in other words, applied research par excellence. Any research work outside this mold should at best be regarded with suspicion, and any citizens involved in it should hardly qualify as contributing to the national effort. Others of our advisers go even further. They tell us that our manpower situation, particularly for combating poverty, ignorance, and disease, is so seriously short of what is required that we should at present concentrate on training at our university institutions only those who are going to fill the vacancies in these areas. Research, whether applied or pure, should, for the time being, be left to expatriates to pursue; our involvement, at best, extending only to formulating the questions to be answered, and, naturally, only to the applied field.

But is this what we really want in East Africa, and is it what is likely to be in our best interests in the long run? Is it possible to pose the right kind of questions without first acquiring the requisite basic attitude? Is it possible for our people to develop as rapidly as we would wish unless some of them are living at the frontier of knowledge? Much more importantly, they must be seen to be employed and practicing there, not only by our population at large, but particularly by our younger generation. New ideas can only be generated through this kind of frontier existence. Imported ideas can be valuable and stimulating, but they become practical only when the local situation has been properly assessed, when they are married to ideas that have been generated through taking into account the totality of the environment.

I would, therefore, reject any notion that the development of the academic spirit is an exercise which we can regard as secondary in East Africa. I consider it as one of the most challenging problems we have in education today: to teach our younger generation to question, with reason, whatever purported facts may be poured into them; to give them the tools, both intellectual and material, with which they can face their own environment and wrest some new information out of it; to teach them first to love knowledge for its own sake, and then draw their attention to the responsibility that they assume, as a result of that knowledge, to the society in which they live. We have to establish a baseline of our own and then map out the direction toward which we should aspire, all along enlisting the help of those more experienced friends who are prepared to come along with us in this exciting exercise. Africa is different from Asia, Europe, or America in the sense that its heart beats at a different tempo, although the blood circulation is the same. But it is necessary to go back a little in our human history in order to appreciate more clearly the problems that face us in the development of the academic spirit.

The Authoritarian Approach

Perhaps it is pertinent to state briefly the view I hold concerning the development of the academic spirit. The whole problem is one of attitudes. One can have a totally acquisitive attitude toward knowledge, without question and without reflection, and it is indeed the line of least resistance to train people to acquire such an attitude. The barrenness of such an approach is now well recognized, but we in East Africa know that we are hardly beginning to scratch the surface in our effort to correct this. On the other hand, it is necessary to develop a reflective, investigative, and experimentally oriented attitude in the fields of both applied and pure knowledge. This is what I would refer to as the academic spirit. If the application of the word "academic" to our national problems has been regarded with suspicion, if there has been a tendency to label the "purely" academic approach a luxury, it is because there has not been a full appreciation of the role played by such an attitude in generating new ideas, in questioning old ones, and in instilling that kind of national confidence in our ability, without which we cannot quickly solve our most pressing and intractable problems.

What then has been our background in this field of the development of academic spirit? East Africa has many tribes, each of which has its own traditional methods of educating the young and the not-so-young. Their methods, however, had many basic features common to them. The elders were the repository of knowledge, and they handed it down with due authority. They knew a great deal about their environment, both from what had been handed down to them and from their own lifetime of experience; within the social and economic framework in which they lived, this knowledge was usually efficacious in dealing with the problems of the day. The attitude, however, was largely authoritarian. There was little room for investigative and experimental approach.

When contact was made with European-style education at the turn of this century, the authoritarian approach to education took what we can now only regard as a more sinister turn! First it was the Bible; and to put the Bible across effectively and quickly, everything African had to be undermined by being referred to as primitive or heathen. Secondly it was education for serving the colonial set-up, and all of us who have passed through it know how destructive of intellectual initiative, how stifling of investigative spirit this was. We had, for instance, two microscopes in our laboratory when we were preparing ourselves for the Cambridge Overseas School Certificates. We were not allowed to touch those microscopes, let alone look into them. Instead, our knowledge of biology consisted of copying out large chunks from J. Arthur Thompson's two-volume text on biology, which we duly tried to commit to memory! It is true that things have improved somewhat since those days, but it would be unrealistic to think that the vast majority of our people today, in whose hands are placed the solutions of some of our basic problems, ever had an opportunity to develop the attitude toward learning and knowledge with which this article is concerned. We are, as a result, handicapped in many areas in getting the kind of intellectual initiative and self-reliance that would meet given situations.

To Instill the Spirit of Inquiry

The problem is basically an educational one. It seems to me important that right from the beginning of a child's education, at the primary school level, he should be introduced to his own environment instead of being cooped up in the classroom all the time, the boredom being relieved only when he is engaged in playing games. At this stage, it would suffice if he could only be made aware of the names of various elements of his habitat, the names of a few major plants and animals, and to some extent their role in the life of his community; the various types of soil and rocks; in short, be able to form an elementary idea of the ecology of his own habitat. No doubt, he will also be involved in a few other classroom subjects, but an important emphasis should be placed on outdoor activities.

As the child proceeds toward his secondary schooling, questions involving "how" should be progressively introduced. There should be an extended build-up in his own knowledge of the inventory of his natural resources. Simple experiments can be introduced. The relationships between the various elements of his own habitat should be explained in as simple a manner as possible.

The secondary school curriculum is a subject which is at the forefront of discussion at the present time. There are debates today as to whether it is wise to have two types of secondary schools: one purely practical in its approach, and whose products, at the end of their schooling, are destined to go out into jobs; the other type of school geared toward producing pupils destined to enter universities or training colleges. Our concern here, however, is that whichever curriculum is being followed, the approach should be such that the pupils will be stimulated to think for themselves, and encouraged to try new pathways to learning.

An important problem here is that of teachers and their training. The primary school teacher is the base on which one eventually builds. His training, therefore, should be imaginative and thorough. Furthermore, he should have effective tools with which to work. How many of our primary school books are geared toward elucidating our own environment and pointing out the gaps in the knowledge of that environment? How many of our teachers have been exposed fully to modern methods of visual aid, and how much of that visual aid has been adapted to our situation? The same problems arise at the secondary school level. If we are to solve the problem of the development of the academic spirit at this level, these problems, and no doubt others that have not been mentioned here, have to be tackled as a matter of priority.

One last point concerning the school program. The problems that arise in the training of teachers with the new outlook are not only confined to the production of new teachers. It is equally important that refresher courses be mounted, so that those who are already in the field should have the benefit of being exposed to this new thinking and the new techniques.

Role of the University

The role of the university in the development of the academic spirit is self-evident. In the teaching of its undergraduates the university should not only present the current status of knowledge; it should also indicate to the students how that knowledge has come about and, at more advanced levels, the direction toward which the frontiers are being extended. The university should be able to send its graduates into the world with tools both intellectual and technical to enable them to learn further. A graduate who leaves the university thinking that he knows all there is to know has missed the point of the university.

But even at the university, in spite of the universality of knowledge, the teaching must be to a large extent projected against the local background if it has to elicit the kind of committed interest that leads to enthusiasm and an urge to ask more questions. There are, of course, subjects that are not amenable to this kind of approach: for example, mathematics. But, by and large, textbooks should be written with local examples as illustrative materials, and research work should be based on local problems.

We are sometimes asked why, in East Africa, we are so keen to Africanize the teaching and research staffs of our institutions. There are many important and urgent reasons for doing this which do not directly concern the present subject. One minor reason, however, which, in the long run, may prove to be as important as any, is the effectiveness of the example shown by our own people, our fellow Africans. The more of our own people we have in universities, displaying the academic spirit with enthusiasm, the more rapidly will this catch on at the lower level and also become self-sustaining at the university level itself.

A PEOPLE APART: THE IK TRIBE [3]

This is written from inside a small, circular mud hut, dark—despite the brilliant sunshine outside—because the door has to be closed to ward off unwelcome visitors who are not deterred even by the eight-foot stockade around the house. There are no windows, but some light and air come in through the eaves, where the thatched roof clears the wall by four or five inches. The floor slopes

[3] "Report from Africa: A People Apart," article by Colin M. Turnbull, associate curator of African ethnology at the American Museum of Natural History. *Natural History.* 75:8-10+. O. '66. Reprinted by permission.

at a ridiculous angle, and the furniture, a bed and two tables made of saplings lashed together with vine, only seems to add to the discomfort. Outside, however, life is even less comfortable, for there is no shelter from the blazing heat, any more than there is from the freezing rain that is likely to follow in an hour or two, blown down the valley by gale-force winds. Distances between villages may not be enormous, but because of the rugged mountain terrain, with ravines a thousand feet deep to be negotiated, it may take a good eight-hour trek to cover as little as ten miles or less, as measured by a straight ruler on a flat map. And even where the land is level for a few hundred yards it is covered with sharp thorns that tear at the arms and legs and, when broken off, penetrate the stoutest soles. Yet, except in moments of temporary despair, it all seems worth while, for although it is like taking blood from the proverbial stone, there is much knowledge to be had from such conditions. The field worker unlucky or unwise enough to have made such a choice is bound to learn not only about the people he is studying but also about himself.

Perhaps even more important, when conditions are as extreme as they are here, in the very northeasternmost corner of Uganda, they make the anthropologist think very carefully about the validity of his results. Here the human environment is just as difficult to cope with as the geographical, and if it is hard for the field worker to accurately and conscientiously survey mountain farmland that frequently slopes at an angle of over seventy degrees, it is even harder for him to maintain his equilibrium while attempting to relate to a people who, while not wishing him any harm, nonetheless wish to strip him of everything he possesses, whether they can conceive of any use for it or not. Nor is it easy to feel at home with a people who regard each other in a similarly covetous light, and who consequently surround themselves with a barrage of deception and ring their homes with tight, virtually impenetrable stockades and thorn fences, dividing brothers from each other and parents from children. While it is true that the anthropologist is no more separated from such people than they are from each other, it is questionable whether he can in a brief year or two ever truly penetrate such formidable defenses and understand just how such a society can survive. Even the hardest head, professing the greatest scientific detachment, can surely not fail to judge harshly when a plump, hearty youth is seen beating a starving, tiny, demented girl for the fun of stealing from her the only food she has seen for a day or two; or when an adult audience roars with laughter as one of their number sneaks food from the bowl of a blind elder as he is eating; or when parents abandon children (or vice versa) to die, not because they could not be fed, but because it would simply take too much trouble—any amount of trouble being too much. The field worker may eventually learn to penetrate the stockades by wriggling through the low doorway on his stomach or on his side, having first announced his intention so as to avoid being attacked, but can he ever penetrate a mentality that looks on with mild amusement as food and water that could save a life are stolen from the dying?

Survival First—Then Understanding

Anthropologists all too often claim to have understood and explained primitive societies *in toto,* as though there was no more to be said on the matter. They present a clearly defined system that would work admirably, like a mechanical model; but also like a mechanical model, it would get nowhere. Perhaps we are all too much concerned with explanation, and too little concerned with understanding. A society like this one, however, defies any explanation, at least for a very long time; none of the standard social systems, of which the theoreticians are so fond and so proud, fit even in part; the field worker is driven, rather like the people he is studying, simply to concentrate on surviving, in the hope that understanding will come, even if system does not.

Anthropology, the study of man, is divided into several different areas in these days of specialization. It is a study of man as a biological entity, as a historical entity, and as a social entity. One of the pities of such specialization is that there is an inevitable tendency to separation, as though man were capable of being rent into discrete parts and still exist. Even within a division, such as social anthropology, there are subdivisions. There are those who seek to answer very specific theoretical problems, and who select a society for study because it illustrates those problems. Others answer a call to solve more empirical problems, such as those posed by the rapid social changes taking place in formerly undeveloped areas. Others, like myself, prefer to undertake a more general quest without any specific expectation except the broadening of our knowledge of human society. We choose a society to study because, in the first place, it is unknown and promises fresh data, and perhaps also because it is generally in line with our own interests, likes, or dislikes.

I like forests, and I am interested in hunters and gatherers, so when casting about for somewhere to go for further research I first chose the Andaman Islands, where the Onge still live (on the Little Andaman) in depleted numbers, but still relatively untouched by civilization. The study would have provided invaluable data for comparison with other hunters and gatherers in similarly forested environments; it would have been of particular interest to me because of my previous work among the pygmy hunters of the Congo. But it was not to be; for various reasons the Indian government refused permission, and with little time left I had to make an alternative choice.

Just then Elizabeth Marshall [Elizabeth M. Thomas], author of *The Harmless People,* returned from northern Uganda where she had been gathering material on the Dodos, one of the great Karimojong peoples. She suggested that since I was so interested in hunters, why not visit the Teuso, who allegedly lived high up in the mountains above the Uganda/Kenya escarpment, and who had first been reported in a very brief note in an academic journal in 1931. She painted a delightful picture of a warm and friendly people, full of fun, whom she had met during their occasional visits to the administrative center of Kaabong, a tiny outpost near the point where Uganda, Kenya, and Sudan all meet in an incredible conglomeration of jagged mountains, arid deserts, and lush, gemlike, and isolated valleys. I reluctantly gave up the idea of a cool forest, and prepared for the hills.

Here again anthropologists differ widely in the kinds of preparations they make. I think all of us read up on whatever literature is available, but in this case it amounted to no more than a few pages. Some then prepare as for any other kind of expedition, purchasing camping equipment and such supplies as cannot be bought locally in the field. Medical supplies have to be carefully assembled, and the necessary inoculations taken. It is all very matter of fact, and when the anthropologist arrives in the field all he has to do is to set up his tent, or tents, assemble all his camping equipment and stores, and then proceed to work much as if he were still in his office, but with an abundant supply of raw material all around. Such an anthropologist deliberately establishes himself outside the community he is studying; some even stay in nearby resthouses or hotels if a town is not too far away. They visit the "field" daily, and pursue a diligent course of study, which they carefully plot as they go along, step by step. They are free from local involvement, emotional or otherwise, and can more easily preserve the intellectual detachment we all aim for. They necessarily miss a great deal by not living in the village with the people, but they claim that their vision, if limited, is clearer by being more objective.

Three Mistakes

There is no right or wrong way; it depends a great deal on the purpose, as well as the nature, of each individual case, and on the personality of the field worker. I prefer to enter a society as completely as possible, for although it becomes impossible to maintain as high a degree of objectivity at the time, one gathers much more material and in much more intimate detail, and this can be treated as objectively as you like when, once out of the field, the material is being analyzed. Of course, it is then too late to fill in any gaps that might result from being too immersed in the subject itself, but on the whole I find the rewards are richer. My previous two major experiences of this kind, in India and in the Congo, had both been immensely fruitful and, at the same time, immensely pleasurable. Minor physical discomforts were quickly obliterated by the constant excitement of discovery and the pleasure of companionship with people who welcomed my desire to learn their ways and were anxious that I understand them well. I saw no reason to think it could be otherwise with the Teuso. That was my first mistake.

The second mistake I made was to assume that the Teuso were hunters until I saw their intensive cultivation, and then to assume that they were farmers. My third mistake, and the greatest, was to assume that these gentle, smiling, friendly looking people who extended such a warm welcome were as gentle and as amicable as they appeared. It took a long time—almost a year—to convince me otherwise.

I arrived at Kaabong at a time when drought was beginning to result in famine. The famine struck the Turkana in Kenya even more heavily, and they were beginning to intensify their raids on the Dodos in Uganda, so that for two weeks the local administration was reluctant to allow me into the danger area. During these two weeks I stayed at Kaabong and met some of the Teuso who filtered down through the mountains in search of food. Two Teuso boys had, during a previous famine, decided to go to the mission school, where they were well fed, as well as well taught. They spoke their own language and Karimojong, which is the lingua franca in this area, and they also knew some English and Swahili. From them, I was able to work up a fairly respectable vocabulary and determine the basic grammatical pattern. I found it relatively easy on paper, but enormously difficult in practice, for the sounds were utterly unlike anything I had ever attempted to make, or had even heard, in a linguistic context. In the course of learning to splutter appropriately, I learned that "Teuso" is only a name applied by the Dodos, and that the tribal name is Ik. Their language is utterly unknown to any of the neighboring tribes, with whom they communicate only in Karimojong. It was unlike any African language known to me, and did not seem to conform to the Sudanic classification it had tentatively been accorded. Perhaps it was the somewhat Bushmanoid appearance of the people that tempted me to see a possible linguistic connection in that direction, but from the outset it was quite plain that the Ik were a people apart from all others in the region, linguistically, physically, and culturally.

Drought and Starvation

As soon as permission came through, I spent a month visiting all the different villages, traveling by jeep as far as practicable, then simply walking or climbing. The effects of the drought had been disastrous. The fields, which had been planted with such evident care and labor, had received just enough rain at the beginning of the season to bring out the young shoots. Then the sun had come to stay in the cloudless sky, burning everything. It burned the crops of the Ik; it also burned the grass that the Dodos needed for their cattle, and it dried up the few water sources that both needed to survive. The outlook was bad, and I was impressed by the cheerfulness with which the Ik accepted the almost certain disaster. Even after the grain that should have been reserved for next year's sowing had been consumed and when there was no longer any chance of rain coming in time to yield a harvest, the Ik, for a reason I could not then understand, remained optimistic. All, that is, except a few old people who were barely strong enough to crawl from their huts to talk. They simply said that they would die, since there was nobody to bring them food, and they were too weak to hunt or gather the wild vegetables that were still about. When I asked if they did not have children to help them, they just laughed —a laugh I quite misunderstood. It was a hollow, hopeless sort of sound that I have heard all too often since, and those who have made it have, as they predicted, mostly died. They did indeed have children, who remained obstinately optimistic and singularly well fed while the skin hung off their parents in long, wrinkled folds, leaving bones to stick out as though in angry protest.

The optimism of the youths, whose plumpness was perhaps comparative but who nonetheless could at least walk upright instead of having to drag themselves along the ground, lay in their knowledge that the drought, two thousand feet down below the escarpment, was even more disastrous for the Turkana. The Turkana, like all Karimojong, live by cattle. They drink the blood and milk of the cows and occasionally eat the flesh of their goats and sheep. The drought became so severe that raids on the Dodos were no longer sufficient remedy, for there simply was no food or water for the vast herds they possessed. Their only recourse, as the Ik well knew, was to climb up the escarpment, invade Uganda, and graze their cattle there.

By then I had decided to make my headquarters near the frontier police post of Pirre, on the side of Mount Morungole, overlooking the Kidepo National Park. There was a cluster of seven Ik villages there, and I had already seen a good deal of the remaining six villages to the east, along the top of the escarpment itself. It was, of course, into Kidepo that the greatest Turkana invasion came, with many thousands of cattle. They drove the Dodos from Pirre; this tiny police post, housed in about a dozen huts, was completely incapable of doing anything against such numbers. The track to Kaabong was barely passable even by jeep, the radio equipment broke down, and the local administration was in a quandary as to what to do, short of calling in the army and creating an international incident.

So the Turkana took possession of Pirre, and I confess that I found them a welcome change, wild and aggressive though they were. They said they had no wish to fight, but only wanted to graze their cattle. They promised they would do no harm if left alone, and although they have probably one of the most unsavory reputations in the whole of Africa, I never doubted their word for an instant, nor did they go back on it even under provocation.

A Talent for Survival

The Ik now displayed their talent for survival. They busied themselves making spears for the Turkana, who had recently been persuaded to surrender theirs as a peace gesture toward the Dodos. For this service they bled the Turkana much as the Turkana bleed their cattle, but with rather less consideration. The Ik began to grow fat again. They then persuaded the Turkana that the Dodos were a menace and began instigating raids between the two, acting first as spies for one side, then for the other, drawing pay in the edible form of cattle from both sides. Ik villages that had never possessed a single goat began to build *bomas* [enclosures for protection against wild beasts] and to fill them with literally hundreds of cattle. They ate these as rapidly as possible, for they knew very well that any attempt to keep them would only result in their being stolen back. The youths continued to put on weight, but the old people remained as thin and emaciated as ever.

The Turkana were eventually forced out by the army, which left the Ik with only the Dodos to prey on, and the Dodos themselves were near starvation. The old people among the Ik began to die, and children, and even some of the youths. The selfishness shown over food was terrible to see, but seemed almost excusable under the circumstances. I myself was driven into hiding every time I wanted to eat, although I had barely enough for myself, since fresh supplies were unobtainable and I had given what I could to the old. Yet I was wary of even biting into a dry biscuit in case someone should hear the crunching and come and demand a share. When people knew anyone was eating, myself included, they came and sat around in a silent, hungry circle, knowing that nothing would be left for them, but hoping. I would have excused them anything during those days, just as I hoped they would excuse me.

The new year came, and with it the first rains in over twelve months. Work in the fields was slow to begin with, for few people had the strength. But the rains brought up edible grasses, wild berries and fruits appeared, and gradually the danger of full-scale starvation receded. Now the crops are well on the way to bringing in a fine harvest, and the wild foods grow in abundance all around. What has not grown, however, is any evidence that the Ik—even in such relatively good times—have any consideration for one another. Food is still the dominant thought; food-getting the dominant activity. And, still, it is each individual for himself. At dawn, children flock out in a large, single, unruly band and scavenge the surrounding countryside for anything that might have come up during the night. The three- to seven- or eight-year-olds are too young to risk going any great distance, where they would stand a better chance. Their older brothers and sisters, having beaten the younger ones to get what they had not yet eaten, go farther out on hunting parties of their own. If caught by their parents, they, in turn, will be beaten and robbed. The adults steal from each other and angrily denounce each other, kinship affording not the slightest bond of mutual respect. A mother will leave her children, even one barely weaned, in care of a father while she goes off to gather for herself, sometimes staying away for a week. Meanwhile the father will go off and leave the children in care of grandparents too old to fend for themselves. To get water, for instance, may well involve a walk of three miles and a descent (and climb, in the reverse direction) of a thousand almost sheer feet. When someone dies, there is no wailing or mourning, merely a great deal of grumbling by the next of kin because of the obligation it places on them to provide ritual purification involving a feast for relatives.

No Trace of Human Compassion

I saw one father hurriedly bury his ten-year-old son by the door of his hut, so as to avoid the expense. The night before, he had beaten his wife to stop her crying when the child died, for by so doing she announced the fact he wished to conceal. All day he sat on a rock and grumbled at his son for dying, at his wife for crying, and at his relatives for demanding a proper burial, including the appropriate feast, to which they would have to be invited. It is, perhaps, at least comforting that the mother cried, but it is the only time I have heard it.

The old people tell stories of better times when, not so long ago, Kidepo Park was theirs to hunt in as they pleased; when the boundaries of the three countries were not subject to armed patrols; and when they could roam at will in search of food and game, instead of being restricted and compressed as they are now. They wonder why the animals in the Park are protected and allowed to live and flourish while they must die. They wonder why their children have abandoned them, for they remember how brothers would all join together, in the old days, to look after their parents. But even the old people, now, have only one concept of good. It is nothing that can be applied to an action, or to a relationship between one human and another; it is only a condition, clearly defined as "having a full stomach." This is the basis of their life, of their law, of their morality. It is a goal that justifies any action except killing, for the Ik never kill. Their legend of origin tells how God gave spears to the Karimojong, together with cattle, so that they have wealth but also the means to bring death. God gave the Ik the digging stick, and told them not to kill. They don't, they just let each other die. Meanwhile they live a life devoid of affection. A woman's attitude to childbirth is that it is a nuisance, another mouth to feed for two or three years. A mother may be amused by her baby, but that is about as close as she seems to get to affection for it. When it is sick or hungry it is simply slapped and cursed as an annoyance. The most equable kind of interpersonal relationship, regardless of kinship, is that of mutual economic reliance, but this is temporary at best and inevitably ends in cheating and mutual recrimination.

A Loveless Society

The tightly stockaded internal divisions, which turn every village into a series of independent fortresses—each occupied by a nuclear family, each with its own single, sometimes booby-trapped private entrance—is sufficient evidence of the state of degeneration into which this society has been thrown by events it cannot understand. Youths have no concept of what their grandparents are talking about when the old folk grumble about the young deserting the old. One, wanting some food I was about to give to an old, old woman, said "Why give it to her? She is going to die anyway." When I said it might make her a little happier meanwhile, he became angry at the waste, for such he considered it.

The economic noose that has been drawn around its neck may be enough to explain the condition into which Ik society has fallen, although even of that I am not yet convinced. It is difficult to understand how, even under such circumstances, a human society can exist and survive as successfully as this one does, devoid of nearly all those qualities that we consider raise us above the level of animals. And however well one may be able to explain the society as it functions at present, is that explanation valid without any understanding of the people themselves? For even simply as people, I still cannot understand the Ik. I cannot bring myself to accept that a loveless society can exist, and constantly look for something I must have missed, fearing all the while that it is not there. The Ik are not a people one can dislike, as much as one dislikes almost everything they do, feeling that even animals would behave with more consideration for each other. One cannot dislike them because they themselves are without the ability to like or dislike, except with regard to the fullness of their bellies: in personal relationships there is a total hiatus.

At the moment it is impossible for me not to be largely subjective. There is always the hope that once I am out of the field, back in familiar and comfortable surroundings, with the leisure and strength to go over every detail in search of the truth, a different truth will emerge. Yet with all this in mind I fear that the truth has already been found. It makes me both angry and sad.

HOW FARES THE WHITE MAN? [4]

Violence in the "model nation" of Nigeria and an uncertain future in Rhodesia are drawing attention to the plight of the white man in still another of Africa's new nations—Kenya.

Here, where a handful of white residents live in a country of millions of Africans, an experiment in "multiracialism" is under way. It is a system that the white government of nearby Rhodesia rejected when it seceded from Britain to try to go it alone.

In theory, Kenya people—white, African, Arab and Asian—are all equal. In reality, what is happening is a steady retreat by white men who have lived and worked here for years.

Yet to be determined is whether, in the end, a white minority can survive in a country dominated by backward and primitive Africans. So far, there have been more disquieting than encouraging signs.

Economic problems are mounting as farm production—basic to Kenya's national income—drops. Government and other services are deteriorating. The political future is far from certain.

The biggest complication, however, is the flight of white farmers and civil servants since this former British colony became free two years ago.

[4] From article, "Whites in Kenya: What's Their Fate?" by Albert J. Meyers. Reprinted from *U.S. News & World Report.* 60:82-3. F. 14, '66.

In the years just before independence, Kenya's white population was 67,000. Today, it has dwindled to 40,000, while the number of Africans stands at 9 million. And the white exodus continues.

Some whites, since independence, have lost their jobs and their homes. Others, unable to adjust to living under an African government, have quit and moved elsewhere. More are finding themselves suddenly living side by side with blacks, sending their children to schools that are fully integrated, and mixing socially with Africans.

All of these changes add up, for the white man in Kenya, to a way of life that suddenly has become very different and even precarious. Many are uncertain and confused. Some, who want to stay in Kenya, are optimistic about the future.

Most uncertain are Kenya's white farmers. In the years before independence, much of Kenya's most fertile land was reserved for whites. They produced nearly 80 per cent of Kenya's cash crops. About 70 per cent of the country's foreign-exchange earnings was derived from the sale of farm products grown by white settlers.

Kenya, unlike many other African countries, has no rich mineral resources to be tapped in developing its economy. It depends largely on its fertile soil to raise crops that can be sold abroad.

Yet, says Alec Ward, director of the Kenya National Farmers' Union, "looking at it over a longish period, I would say that eventually most white farmers in Kenya will be gone."

A Question of Money

Since independence, the Kenya government has been carrying out a policy of replacing white farmers with Africans. Today, only about 900 white farm families, out of an original 3,200, remain. Many still here want to leave. Question is whether the government can find the money to buy them out.

Some seven hundred white farmers already have been bought out with funds put up by Britain, the World Bank and the British Commonwealth Development Fund. These purchases acquired about 1 million acres of the 2.5 million acres which used to be reserved for whites. Now, funds for this purpose are running out.

Some farmers in an area northwest of Nairobi have been plagued by hordes of African "squatters," who move onto the white farms, grow a few crops of their own and refuse to leave. Many farmers have had their cattle stolen.

Britain has recommended a slowdown in the policy of buying out white farmers and replacing them with Africans. Officially, the Kenya government opposes the idea of a slowdown. But there is some evidence that the African government would like to find a way, gracefully, to go more slowly. The transition period is having some bad effects on the economy.

Kenya's rate of growth, for example, is not up to expectations. This is seen as due, in part at least, to economic losses stemming from the changeover from efficient farming by whites to less-efficient farming by blacks.

The country's economy grew by 2 per cent during 1965, against a forecast of 4 per cent. [Subsequent years have seen much higher growth rates.—Ed.] At the same time, Kenya's population keeps increasing by 3 per cent every year. Under these conditions, Kenya keeps falling behind, not pushing ahead, in its efforts to improve the lives of its nine million Africans.

Losses laid to the changeover in farm ownership have been aggravated by serious drought, a drop in world prices for Kenya's products, plus a plague of crop diseases. Farm revenue fell from $155 million in 1964 to $140 million last year [1965].

Coffee output plummeted to 36,000 tons, from 43,500 tons a year ago. Production of tea, sisal and pyrethrum, other major exports, also diminished.

Corn, Kenya's staple food and normally an export crop is having to be imported from the United States.

In what used to be the white highlands, many farmhouses stand vacant. In Nairobi, office space is going begging as businesses which depended on the white farmers decline.

At Nanyuki, a small town near Mount Kenya, only 150 whites remain and the local hunt club has had to be dissolved for lack of members. The Nanyuki Club once was one of five English hunt clubs in Kenya. Two remain.

Many Whites Are Adjusting

There are, on the other hand, not a few whites—including farmers—who say they are reasonably well adjusted to life under an African government, even if they don't like it.

One of these is Michael Rowbotham, a bitterly anti-African farmer before independence. Mr. Rowbotham, a Scot, is also one of Kenya's "white hunters." He is staying on, still farming and hunting.

In the period just before Rhodesia unilaterally declared its independence, a group of white farmers in Kenya called on their Rhodesian counterparts to adjust to black rule, rather than secede. The group was headed by Lord Delamere, a member of one of Kenya's pioneer families.

"I have no intention of leaving," says Lord Delamere.

Similarly, Sir Michael Blundell, a former government minister, is staying on at a farm northwest of Nairobi. Sir Michael came to Kenya forty years ago.

On balance, however, there probably is more pessimism than optimism in Kenya's white farming community.

Many white farms are up for sale at prices that would have brought buyers quickly a few years ago. One farmer recently advertised his 274-acre farm, completely fenced and padlocked, with a six-room house and a "very high grade" Jersey herd, all for $18,500.

The Kenya government is looked upon by American diplomatic officials as a friend of the West. It encourages private enterprise, condemns communism and counts principally on Britain and the United States to provide the help needed to develop the country.

Jomo Kenyatta, Kenya's president and a one-time terrorist, is regarded by Westerners here now as an "elder statesman" in African affairs. His government refused to join with other, more radical, African states in breaking relations with Britain over Rhodesia.

"We used to hate Kenyatta's guts," says a white farmer in Nakuru. "Now he's probably the best chance we've got. Besides, we hate to think of what will come after him."

It is this thought that frightens many whites—what will happen in the future after Kenyatta departs? Even now, some whites have lost their government jobs although they had fulfilled the requirement of taking out Kenya citizenship.

Jobs for Whites

At present, the Kenya government has one white minister, a South African by origin, who heads the agriculture department. The top-ranking officer in the Kenya army is an Englishman. The deputy commissioner of police is a white man, but his chief is an African.

In the Kenya civil service, some 1,500 white men still hold important jobs, their salaries paid by the British government. None of these whites, even if born and raised in Kenya, expects to hold on to his job after he has trained an African to replace him.

In the business world, practically all top jobs are held by white men or Asians. Many companies, under pressure of the government, have given jobs to Africans. Some blacks now serve on the boards of directors of white companies. Others have high-sounding titles but little responsibility.

A returning visitor notices changes. The principal hotel in Mombasa, Kenya's main seaport, used to have white receptionists, Asian cashiers, Italians as head waiter and bartender. All of these jobs now are held by Africans. A deterioration in services is noticeable.

Without aid from abroad, Kenya clearly would have little chance of succeeding. Besides paying the wages of British civil servants, Britain pumps an annual sum into the national budget, provides the money to build roads, schools and hospitals, and pays the education fees for hundreds of Kenya students in Britain. More than half a billion dollars in British money has been poured into East Africa since 1945, and the end is not in sight.

The United States, too, puts a lot of money into Kenya—$42 million in grants since 1948. Enter a Kenya school and the teacher you meet is likely to be an American whose salary is paid by the United States Government.

U.S. businessmen are looking more and more favorably upon Kenya as a place in which to invest. There now are more than fifty companies operating out of Nairobi, an increase since independence of twenty-nine firms. Total U.S. investment in Kenya, including joint operations with European companies, is more than $80 million.

Up to the present, Kenya's white population has not had clear sailing since the introduction of a black government. The white farmer, particularly, has been hard hit. But, since the Mau Mau uprising was put down in 1960, Kenya's whites have not had to contend with hordes of murderous Africans, as whites in the Congo have. Many whites in Kenya believe they can continue to live here without serious trouble.

Kenya, for all its problems, strikes a visitor as having a good chance—under its present government—of keeping racial minorities from being completely submerged in a sea of black Africans.

INDIAN COMMUNITY UNDER PRESSURE [5]

A deep feeling of anxiety bordering in some places on panic has developed among the Indian communities in East Africa.

In Kenya, Uganda and Tanzania they are under heavy pressure from the governments to "Africanize"—to find some quick way of handing over their long domination of commerce to Africans or to suffer the wrath of the authorities or the people, or perhaps both.

The Indians, approaching 400,000 in number in the region, are nearly all descendants of artisans and laborers the British brought over toward the end of the nineteenth century to build the railway from Mombasa to the interior.

In Tanzania the elimination of Indian traders has begun in earnest. The government is not giving out figures, but well over one hundred expulsion orders have been issued to Indian traders who do not have Tanzanian passports. . . .

[5] From "Indians Are Upset in Eastern Africa," by Lawrence Fellows, staff correspondent. New York *Times.* p 25. F. 5, '67. © 1967 by The New York Times Company. Reprinted by permission.

Filling a Vacuum

While the British never really yielded much control over production of primary products in their colonies, the Indians moved swiftly and easily into the vacuum in trade to become importers, wholesalers and retailers.

The tight-knit communities still control about four fifths of the commerce in East Africa, with each community enforcing a certain amount of business discipline and ethics on itself. The system has made it difficult for Africans without experience and capital to break in.

The result has been that the Africans, disappointed that their economic status has not improved with independence, have directed their envy and anger against the aloof and easily identifiable Indian communities.

Those Indians who filled the lower levels of the civil service have also been falling victims to Africanization since the three territories achieved independence.

Five of the traders being ousted by Tanzania on two months' notice—they are the country's only large-scale pot makers—claimed possession of work permits good for two years more. Four are British subjects and one is an Indian. All their children were born in Tanzania and are registered as citizens. Their businesses, they said, are fifty to sixty years old.

An article by Lawi Sijaona, Tanzania's minister of home affairs, in *The Nationalist,* official daily newspaper of the Tanganyika African National Union, the country's only political party, said that foreigners were not needed to do jobs Tanzanians could do. He mentioned barbers, shoemakers and a long list of others.

"I call on all people in these categories to start packing," he said.

In Kenya and Uganda, the pressures have been building up also.

The Kenya government is holding secret hearings on a bill aimed at speeding the pace of Africanization in commerce. Tom Mboya, minister of economic planning and development, has warned that unless Indians open up their businesses, including family-run concerns, to Africans, a serious situation will arise.

The *East African Standard,* an English-language newspaper in Nairobi, said editorially last week that the crisis was already here —that before long many ethnic Indians would be forced to leave East Africa, some holding British or Indian passports, others no passports at all. [This warning bore fruit early in 1968, when thousands of Indians were expelled from Kenya. See editor's note at end of "East Africa—An Overview," in Section I, above.—Ed.]

V. EAST AFRICA'S TROUBLED NEIGHBORS

EDITOR'S INTRODUCTION

The normal trials and tribulations of independence are one thing; the added strains resulting from external pressures are quite another. Today East Africa is subject to both. Much of the rest of Africa is in or near upheaval. In the past several years, military coups have ousted leaders in Togo, the Congo, Dahomey, the Central African Republic, Nigeria, and Ghana. North of Uganda, in the Sudan, a race war is raging which could eventually spill over into the racially mixed societies of East Africa itself.

To the west the troubled Congo seems in a perpetual state of upheaval bordering on civil war. To the south are the white-ruled states of Southern Rhodesia, Mozambique, and South Africa, whose racial policies constitute a threat to every black African nation. And last but far from least are the pressures generated by the cold war, with its three-way intrigue involving Washington, Moscow, and Peking. By virtue of its geographic location and political vulnerability, East Africa is highly sensitive to all these pressures.

The six articles of this section are designed to acquaint the reader with East Africa's troubled environment. In the first article a professor of African studies summarizes the difficulties in Africa's key trouble spots, including the problem posed by Southern Rhodesia since its unilateral declaration of independence from British rule. Next, a writer and lecturer on African affairs describes some of the causes for dissension within the Organization of African Unity and the reasons for that group's decline in recent years. The special problems faced by neighboring Zambia, the Congo, and the Sudan are dealt with in the next three articles. And in the last, Under Secretary of State Nicholas deB. Katzenbach sets forth an American view of the unique contribution that all of Africa can make to the world.

AFRICA'S TROUBLE SPOTS: A SURVEY [1]

Africa's importance in world affairs derives from its political presence in the international arena, not from its economic strength or military power. The African states account for almost one third of the membership of the UN. With a total population half that of India, Africa has thirty-nine times as many votes in the UN General Assembly and, potentially, constitutes the most formidable voting block in the UN and other international agencies. Moreover, Africa has three seats in the Security Council, and there is a possibility that the next secretary-general of the UN will come from Africa.

Thus, in a number of ways, the balance of underdeveloped-area political power seems to be shifting somewhat from Asia to Africa. This fact has not been lost on the great powers or the lesser powers. And the competition for African support in the UN has been strong and intense on a number of issues.

External Political Issues: The Two Chinas

In recent years the admission of Communist China to the UN has turned largely on the vote of African states. Both mainland China and Nationalist China (Taiwan) have been engaged in a highly competitive race to win their votes. The Nationalist Chinese have had a good deal of success with their foreign aid programs in Africa, particularly with technical assistance in the fields of rice cultivation, raising of garden vegetables, development of the fishing industry and small-scale shipbuilding. Communist China, drawing upon greater resources, has met with mixed results in its foreign aid programs centering around the provision of factories and commodities. Principal recipients of Communist Chinese aid, such as Guinea and pre-coup Ghana in West Africa, and Tanzania in East Africa, have apparently been somewhat less than happy with its quality and usefulness.

[1] From *New States of Africa*, by Arnold Rivkin, lawyer, economic adviser, author of *African Presence in World Affairs* and *Africa and the West*. (Headline Series. no 183) Foreign Policy Association. 345 E. 46th St. New York 10017. '67. p 39-51. Reprinted by permission.

Communist China, in keeping with Premier Chou En-lai's proclamation during his first state visit to Africa that the area was "ripe for revolution," has also sought to export Communist Chinese political doctrine and "wars of national liberation." The result has been vigorously outspoken criticism of Peking's interference by the OCAM [Organisation Commune Africaine et Malgache], composed largely of former French territories, and by the new military governments of the Central African Republic, Dahomey and Ghana. From time to time other African governments have denounced Chinese intrusion in their internal affairs. In East Africa, Kenya has several times complained about the discovery of hidden caches of Chinese arms on its territory and the flow of Chinese funds to the political opposition in the country. President H. Kamuza Banda of Malawi has accused China of supporting the political opposition in attempts to overthrow his government.

Peking's relations with the area are complicated by the fact that the United States has been actively engaged in attempting to find African support for its policy of excluding Communist China from the UN. On the other hand, France, since its reversal of position a few years ago and its recognition of Communist China, has withdrawn any opposition it may have voiced earlier to recognition by the French-speaking African states.

Impact of Sino-Soviet Rift

Thus, the highly important and quite remote issue of the two Chinas has found in Africa an important new arena. So, too, has the related issue of the Sino-Soviet split. As a result of their struggle for ascendancy in the Communist world, both Communist China and the Soviet Union have been increasingly engaged in competition for support. One direct consequence has been a marked lessening of Soviet efforts to influence African states in favor of Peking's admission to the UN.

The case of Somalia perhaps best illustrates the competition between the two Communist superstates. When the Republic of Somali was unable to obtain arms for a major expansion of its armed forces in connection with its continuing violent border disputes with both Ethiopia and Kenya, the Somali government turned to Communist China for assistance, and Peking was only too ready to supply it. However, because of the strategic location of the Republic of Somali, the Soviet Union decided to outbid the Chinese and, in the process, the West in both the provision of arms and economic assistance. Today, the Somali armed forces are largely Russian-equipped and trained, and a significant part of its economic aid now also comes from the Soviet bloc.

The Sino-Soviet competition in Somalia also affects other African states and Western countries. . . . Somalia has been over the last several years engaged in a continuing series of border incidents with its two near-neighbors, Ethiopia and Kenya. In view of the fact that Ethiopia obtains the bulk of its arms from the United States and Kenya receives the bulk of its arms from the United Kingdom, the mounting warfare between the Republic of Somali and its two neighbors, which now have a common defense pact, illustrates the dangerous cold-war and chain-reaction implications of external involvement in volatile intra-African situations.

The Congo Crises

In strictly cold-war terms the Congo (Kinshasa) and Guinea present interesting examples of the confrontation of Western and Communist influences in tropical Africa. In the Congo the confrontation has perhaps been the most serious of any in Africa, and the most volatile. The first confrontation took place soon after Congolese independence (June 30, 1960) in the confused atmosphere of the mutiny of the Congolese national army and the ensuing intervention by Belgium in its former colony. The United States supported the UN peace-keeping force in the Congo, which in its early phase was criticized by the Communist bloc and some of the more radical nationalist states for seemingly supporting President Joseph Kasavubu in his struggle with the more radical Prime Minister Patrice Lumumba. The Communist bloc tended to operate outside of the UN framework in support of the prime minister. The prime minister's fall from power led to the ouster of various Communist bloc embassies by the then chief of staff of the army, Colonel Joseph Mobutu, who seized power for the first time.

The second confrontation in the Congo was more sharply drawn, with a somewhat different set of leading characters. In mid-1964 widespread rebellions engulfed a large part of the eastern and northern parts of the Congo. They were apparently supported by Communist Chinese sources in neighboring African countries, primarily in Burundi and the Congo (Brazzaville). Communist weapons, particularly of Chinese origin, were supplied to the rebel forces. Meanwhile, following the withdrawal from the Congo of the UN peace-keeping force at the end of June 1964, the United States became the principal supplier of military assistance to the central government in Leopoldville [later renamed Kinshasa]. Included in the assistance were a small number of American aircraft which were flown by Cuban exiles. In this connection it is interesting to note that Castroite Cubans were from time to time reported to be present as advisers and trainers of various rebel forces.

The Guinea Case

The Guinea case has been far less dramatic and far less volatile. After Guinea's vote for independence from the French Community in the September 1958 constitutional referendum, the French reacted bitterly and withdrew completely from Guinea. Other Western nations, following the French lead, remained aloof. Guinea reacted, partly because of the logic of events and partly because of its ideological predispositions, by turning to the east and developing close relationships with various Communist nations. Guinea received arms, economic and technical assistance from them. This state of affairs continued until the end of 1961, when the Soviet ambassador was ousted for interfering in the internal affairs of the country. Guinea then sought *rapprochement* with the West, particularly with the United States.

Starting in late 1965, the pendulum started to swing again the other way. Guinea broke its brief *rapprochement* with France by accusing France of conspiring with neighboring states to overthrow the Guinean government. Later, in 1966, the close relationship which had grown up between Guinea and the United States cooled off as Guinea became increasingly critical of African states with which the United States was friendly and of United States policy elsewhere. At the same time the intimacy of Guinea's relationship with the Soviet bloc and Communist China increased.

Thus the West and the East have been engaged in a game of musical chairs in Guinea in large part of a preemptive nature. Each has sought to preclude the other from developing a dominant position in the small West African state. The fortunes of both have varied as various factions within the single party in the one-party state have altered their positions and achieved a momentary ascendancy.

Lesser External Powers in Africa

Among the lesser powers perhaps the most dramatic competition for support of African states is to be found in the Arab-Israeli situation. Israel has been quite successful in developing diplomatic, political and economic relationships with the new African states. Through trade and aid Israel has developed ties with Nigeria, Sierra Leone, Senegal, the Ivory Coast, Kenya and many other sub-Saharan African countries, and these ties have permitted Israel to circumvent the Arab states' boycott around its borders. As a consequence, on most issues in the last four or five years Israel has had the warm support of many African states in the UN. The Arab states have from time to time sought to supplant or compete with the Israeli programs in the area, but their efforts have met with limited results. Their principal political success was the . . . Security Council resolution severely criticizing Israel for its retaliatory raid on Jordan in November 1966. The Arabs were able to persuade the two African members of the Security Council to take the lead in introducing the critical resolution, which all of the Security Council members, except New Zealand, felt it necessary to support.

From the examples given, it can be seen that the multifaceted presence of the new African states has created a new dimension in international political affairs. On the one hand, there has been a marked competition among external powers for their support in the UN and the international arena generally. On the other hand, various African situations reflecting either internal weakness and instability or involving competition have attracted or ensnared external powers into African conflicts or disputes, such as the triangular Somalian, Ethiopian and Kenyan territorial controversy.

Africa's Economic Presence

Eurafrican trade, investment and aid are the most distinctive and important aspects of tropical Africa's economic presence in world affairs. Almost without exception, the new states look to their former colonial rulers as the principal source of trade, investment and aid, and retain their membership in the currency areas to which they were linked before independence.

Liberia, which has no colonial past, uses the United States dollar as a medium of foreign exchange and is a member of the dollar area. Ethiopia's currency is independent and backed by Ethiopian reserves of gold and hard currencies. Both Liberia and Ethiopia have important trade, investment and aid ties with the United States. There are major U.S. investments in Liberian rubber plantations and iron ore mines.

The various countries of sub-Saharan Africa have tried to diversify their economic relations and, in particular, to develop new trading partners and new sources of external aid. Nigeria, the Congo (Kinshasa) and Kenya have been developing new economic ties with the United States. Others, such as Guinea and Mali have developed new economic relationships with the Soviet bloc and Communist China. And as we have already noted, a fair number of countries in the area have developed economic relationships with the state of Israel, as have several with Japan, a newcomer to the African field.

By and large, however, the Eurafrican ties remain paramount and have been consolidated for the eighteen African states in the area which are associate members of the European Economic Community (EEC). Under the original Treaty of Rome signed in 1957, and the more recent Yaoundé Convention, they have developed a series of preferential trade, aid and investment relations with the six European countries forming the EEC.

Summing up—on the world scene tropical Africa is not a major area for trade or investment. It does not, with a few exceptions, loom large in terms of the total trade and investments of even the European powers. The Belgian trade and investment relationship with the Congo (Kinshasa) is an exception. As for France, only its dealings with the Ivory Coast, Senegal and Gabon have any particular significance. To the United States and the Soviet Union, the area is one of minor economic significance.

In the foreign aid field the area has been the principal recipient of French foreign aid and an important recipient of British foreign aid. The Development Fund of the European Economic Community, to which the six European members contribute, has also been a source of major external aid. Tropical Africa has received the smallest amount of aid of any geographic area in the world from the United States and has also received only limited aid from the Soviet Union. In individual cases the United States has provided important quantities of aid—to Nigeria for its first post-independence economic development plan; to Guinea in order to weaken its links to the Soviet bloc; and to the Congo (Kinshasa) as a consequence of the continuing crisis in that country. Similarly, the Soviet Union has provided significant quantities of aid to such countries as Guinea, pre-coup Ghana and the Republic of Somali.

The economic importance of Africa can be expected to increase in time. Trading and investment opportunities have been opening up and are likely to grow. There is not likely, however, to be any dramatic change in the area's economic importance in the near future in view of the widespread political instability and internal economic difficulties.

Africa's Military Presence

Africa's military presence has been largely irrelevant to problems of the world balance of military power. It has not and is not likely to affect significantly major international issues or even intra-African issues, such as the continuing defiance of the UN by the minority white Rhodesian government, the struggle for the "liberation" of the Portuguese territories in southern Africa, the disputed South African mandate of South-West Africa and the fate of the nonwhite peoples of South Africa. If anything, the military weakness of the area has been a source of frustration to the militant states seeking to use direct force to resolve these intra-African issues, while at the same time it has buttressed the position of the "white redoubts" in southern Africa.

Despite the military weakness of the area in world terms, in regional terms the African military presence is important and is growing. And it is this latter fact which gives it its principal importance on the world scene.

The border conflicts and small local wars which we have earlier alluded to can spread like a brush fire and involve external powers. Endemic political instability in African countries and the prominent internal role of the military have been factors in promoting the internal rebellions and military coups which have had a real potential for attracting the intervention of external powers.

The nonstop political turmoil in the Congo (Kinshasa) has involved a number of major external powers, to say nothing of other African states which have special links of one sort or another with non-African powers. So, too, in 1964 military mutinies in East Africa drew in the United Kingdom and the military coup in Gabon drew in France. In Nigeria the military coups of January and July 1966 and the continuing political crisis with its attendant violence have led to various proposals for calling in external military forces, primarily from the United Kingdom.

The Arms Race

The arms race in various parts of Africa, already referred to, and the internal dominance of military forces in a number of African states have also drawn external powers into the volatile political scene. Many of the sub-Saharan African states rely on their former colonial rulers for military equipment, supplies and training. In fact, many of the former French territories have defense pacts with France. Under just such a pact France interceded in the Gabon to restore the overthrown government of President Leon M'Ba. As noted earlier, some of the African countries have turned to the

Soviet bloc for military equipment, supplies and training. Some have also turned to Communist China. In a few instances countries, such as the Congo (Kinshasa), have come to rely on the United States for their military assistance. In addition, the United States has long been the principal supplier of military assistance to Liberia, as well as to Ethiopia, ever since the Korean war, when Ethiopia provided the only African troops for the UN force in Korea.

Finally, "wars of national liberation" and attempts at subversion of the governments of the new states have been supported by clandestine shipments of foreign arms, frequently from the Soviet bloc or Communist China, sometimes through the intermediary of African states, such as pre-coup Ghana. These have, on occasion, led to any number of dangerous incidents with external implications. Hidden shipments of Chinese Communist arms discovered in Kenya led to a period of acute recriminations between Kenya and its two neighbors, Tanzania and Uganda, and also between Kenya and Communist China. So, too, a mysterious arms shipment, reportedly of Communist origin, apparently intended for subversive activities in the former Italian territory of Eritrea, which is now part of Ethiopia, was intercepted in the Sudan and led to recrimination within the Sudan as well as between Ethiopia and the Sudan. There has also been a whole series of underground shipments of arms of Communist origin from Burundi and the Congo (Brazzaville) into the northern and eastern parts of the Congo (Kinshasa) for support of various rebel movements. The direct result was increased requests to the United States and other Western powers for additional military assistance to the central government to combat the rebels.

Thus, for the outside world the significance of the African military presence is the danger of involving outside powers in a variety of situations arising from the internal political weakness of the new states and their political rivalries and disputes. As the number of new states continues to increase in the area and the number of boundary lines increases proportionately, the danger of external involvement will continue to mount.

The Rhodesian Problem

The continuing political crisis involving Rhodesia has been a major issue for all the independent states of Africa for the last several years. One of the few issues on which they agree is their antipathy for the controlling minority white government of Rhodesia and their advocacy of external intervention to establish a majority (black) African government in the territory. In an unprecedented action, late in 1966, the UN Security Council voted at British request to impose selective economic sanctions on the rebellious Rhodesian government. The sanctions require the members of the UN to ban the import of the principal exports of Rhodesia and the sale to it of arms, military equipment and petroleum. Portugal and South Africa have announced that they do not intend to comply with the Security Council resolution, which made no provision for enforcing the sanctions. There is also a serious question as to the extent to which neighboring Zambia, given its dependence on Rhodesia for much of its manufactured imports and coal, will be able or willing to impose such a ban.

The new African states are also interested in the independence struggle taking place in Portuguese Guinea. There also has been growing interest in the possible accession to independence of French Somaliland and the Spanish Sahara. However, because of conflicting claims of various African states, these territories have not been rallying points against colonialism and outside domination in the same way that Rhodesia and Portuguese Guinea have been.

Southern Africa

Although they are outside of the area under discussion, the independence movements in Portuguese Mozambique and Angola, the *apartheid* issue in South Africa and the related problem of the future status of the League of Nations mandate in South-West Africa have been the subject of widespread concern to all African states, and particularly to those nearby. Tanzania has been actively involved in the anti-Portuguese struggle in Mozambique, as the base for the latter's rebel forces, and the Congo (Kinshasa) has been increasingly drawn into a similar situation in Angola, as the base for the rebel Angolan government-in-exile.

The issues involving Portuguese Africa, South-West Africa and South Africa itself have dominated almost every session of the UN for the past two or three years and are likely to continue to do so until some sort of resolution of the problems they present is found. In 1966 the issue of the future of South-West Africa reached a climax when the International Court of Justice (World Court), in a much-disputed decision, ruled by an 8-7 vote on procedural grounds against the complaining states of Liberia and Ethiopia.

The two black African states had argued that the South African policy of racial discrimination or separate racial development, which was introduced into the territory of South-West Africa, was a breach of South Africa's mandate to develop the area in the best interests of the local inhabitants. Frustrated by the adverse decision of the World Court, the African states turned to the UN General Assembly for action. The Assembly adopted a resolution in October 1966, with only South Africa and Portugal voting against and the United Kingdom, France and Malawi abstaining, which declared that South Africa, because of its racial practices in South-West Africa, had forfeited its mandate and that the UN would assume "responsibility" for the territory. Following a report by a fourteen-member committee, the General Assembly on May 19 [1967] adopted a resolution establishing an eleven-member council to administer the territory until independence. The Western and Communist bloc nations (except for Yugoslavia), which abstained from voting, believe that the resolution cannot be implemented, since South Africa has indicated it will not comply willingly with the resolution.

South Africa has denounced the October 1966 resolution as beyond its authority and illegal and refused to recognize it in any way as binding. Many UN member countries are perplexed as to what the UN can or should do next in the face of South Africa's resistance to implementation of the resolution. The possibility of invoking economic and military sanctions has been mentioned by some UN members, particularly the African countries, as the ultimate weapon to which the UN might turn. But realistically such sanctions are most unlikely to be authorized by the Security Council, particularly in light of the abstention of two of the permanent members of the Security Council, Britain and France, each of which has a veto on Council resolutions.

DISSENSION IN THE ORGANIZATION OF AFRICAN UNITY [2]

A tragic revelation of the last few years was the inability of the Organization of African Unity (OAU) to live up to the high expectations held for it. Although every head of state in Africa had been quick to profess undying faith in the principles of the OAU's charter, virtually none was willing, or perhaps able, to live up to them. Leaders who had signed the charter in 1963, and who rarely missed an opportunity to pose as its champions, did not hesitate to traduce either the letter or the spirit of the charter when it was advantageous to do so. Nowhere was this discrepancy between public profession and private practice more evident than in the unwillingness of the various members to abide by Article III of the charter, which pledged them to refrain from interfering in the internal affairs of other states. The temptation to meddle proved irresistible to most African heads of state. Nkrumah spent millions financing terrorist groups carrying out subversion in Cameroun, Togo, Niger, and the Ivory Coast. Presidents Julius Nyerere of Tanzania, Milton Obote of Uganda, Ahmed Ben Bella of Algeria, and Modibo Keita of Mali openly gave aid to the rebels who sought to overthrow the Congo (Leopoldville [now Kinshasa]) legal government. Yet all of these men still unabashedly proclaimed themselves supporters of the OAU.

The effectiveness of the OAU was also reduced, very soon after its creation, when it came under the control of its more extreme members. The so-called revolutionary bloc—consisting of the United Arab Republic, Algeria (under Ben Bella), Guinea, Mali, Tanzania, and Ghana (under Nkrumah)—set the tone of the organization. Under their influence, the organization became not so

[2] From *African Ferment: 1966*, by Victor D. Du Bois, a writer and lecturer on African affairs. (West Africa Series. v 9) American Universities Field Staff. Reports Service. 366 Madison Ave. New York 10017. '66. p 6-11. Reprinted by permission.

much an instrument for promoting African unity as a forum for the most violent sort of anticolonial and anti-Western diatribes. Unable to have their way at the United Nations, these more radical African states used the OAU to thrust themselves on the international political scene. Convinced that they alone had the solution to the ills that plagued Africa, they made the OAU a rostrum from which they proposed dubious programs.

Fiasco Over Rhodesia

Their irresponsible leadership came to a dramatic climax in May . . . [1966] over the Rhodesian crisis. Impatient with what they termed Prime Minister Wilson's reluctance or incompetence to resolve it, the radical bloc, at a meeting of the OAU Council of Foreign Ministers in Addis Ababa, pushed through a resolution calling for member states to sever relations with the United Kingdom if Wilson did not soon bring Prime Minister Ian Smith to heel. Governments which in a more sober frame of mind would never have contemplated such a step allowed themselves to be swept along by the fiery rhetoric of the revolutionary leaders. By the time they realized the folly of their action, it was too late; their votes had been cast.

As the OAU's deadline approached, it became unmistakably clear even to the most obdurate African leaders that the British government would not succumb to such pressures, even supposing it were able to force the issue with Mr. Smith. Some states disavowed their hasty vote; others simply ignored it. A few—Tanzania, Algeria, Ghana, and Guinea—went ahead for the sake of principle and broke their ties with Great Britain. Theirs was at best a symbolic gesture and only brought ridicule on the OAU.

Belatedly, the moderates realized that the OAU was being undermined from within by the radical states, and they launched a heavy and sustained counterattack to wrest control from them. In the forefront of this attack was Félix Houphouët-Boigny, President of the Ivory Coast and the unquestioned leader of the moderate states of French-speaking black Africa. Acting through the Council of the Entente [a loose economic grouping of five West African states, of which the Ivory Coast is a member] and the Organisation Commune Africaine et Malgache (OCAM), both of which he had helped to establish, Houphouët rallied the moderate states to his point of view. This view was, simply, that moderate Africa should and could be heard within the OAU and other world councils as much as the revolutionary states.

Emerging from what some observers had termed its "splendid isolation," the Ivory Coast became, so to speak, the militant state of the moderate bloc. Africa's old division into two rival camps, the revolutionaries and the moderates, became more pronounced. A contest was under way, the immediate objective being control of the OAU, but the ultimate aim, of course, being to determine how independent Africa should develop—by evolution or revolution. In such a contest it was essential to have as many allies as possible, and Houphouët, realizing this, did not limit himself to soliciting support from the French-speaking states of black Africa. He also cultivated the late Prime Minister Abubakar Tafawa Balewa of Nigeria, admitted Congo (Leopoldville)—under Moise Tshombe—into the OCAM, and even sought to attach Ethiopia, Liberia, Tunisia, and Morocco to the moderate bloc. Gradually the moderate states began to return blow for blow the thrusts directed against them by such men as Kwame Nkrumah and Sékou Touré.

Battle for Control

The battle for control of the OAU was fought in chancelleries and conference rooms all over Africa. It involved radio and press campaigns and repeated visits and confidential exchanges between African heads of state. As the moderate states gradually coordinated their policies and consolidated their forces, the tide of battle turned in their favor. They and not the revolutionary states began to carry the day in the councils of the OAU. When rival Congolese delegations, one representing the Kasavubu government and the other representing the rebel forces, showed up at Addis Ababa in March 1965 to represent the Congo, the Kasavubu delegation was recognized. Nkrumah had assured the OCAM leaders that he would cease trying to subvert their governments and would expel antimoderate exiles from his country; and when he failed to honor these pledges, the OCAM leaders, virtually en masse, boycotted the OAU summit conference at Accra in November 1965. After Nkrumah's overthrow, when Guinea tried to bar the seating of the new Ghanaian delegation representing General Ankrah's government, the proposal was overwhelmingly voted down. The net result of this struggle, inevitably, was the weakening of the OAU.

Another debilitating factor was the unwillingness of most member states to make use of OAU machinery to resolve their disputes or to promote programs of common action. In part, their reluctance was due to the fact that the administrative machinery of the OAU was cumbersome, the lines of authority blurred, and the procedures slow and tortuous; but it must also be attributed to the conviction, held by African leaders generally, of the righteousness of their positions and an unwillingness to have the merits of their claims debated by a disinterested body.

The OAU's orientation toward continental rather than regional problems led member states either to resort to direct negotiation with the party concerned or to work through regional organizations which could get things done more expeditiously. Thus the Council of the Entente, the OCAM, and the Customs Union of Equatorial States came to be more important to the French-speaking states than the OAU. Then, too, because so few states actually met their financial obligations, the OAU was often on the verge of bankruptcy.

Disagreement Over China

On a trip to East Africa in 1964, Chinese Premier Chou En-lai remarked that "the revolutionary perspectives are excellent in the African Continent." At the time the observation seemed warranted: A leftist revolution had swept Zanzibar. Rebel forces were in control of almost half of the ex-Belgian Congo, and across the river, in the former French Congo, dissatisfied workers had overthrown the conservative and pro-Western regime of President Fulbert Youlou and installed in its place an anti-Western government friendly to China. Senegal, Dahomey, the Central African Republic, and Mauritania had all decided to sever diplomatic relations with Formosa and to establish ties with Peking. African leaders strongly sympathetic to the Chinese Communists were in power in the United Arab Republic, Algeria, Guinea, Mali, Ghana, Tanzania, and Burundi.

But then China's fortunes began to change. Moderate African leaders, disturbed by Chou En-lai's statement and uneasy over China's ultimate designs on Africa, began to be more wary. Chinese meddling in certain African states inspired widespread fears. Burundi expelled the Chinese ambassador for interference in the country's internal affairs, and Kenya expelled Chinese newsmen on a similar charge. Following the coups in Dahomey, the Central African Republic, and Ghana, these countries severed relations with Peking.

Despite such momentary setbacks, China is still a major worry to many African leaders. Some of them, like President Félix Houphouët-Boigny of the Ivory Coast, President Hamani Diori of Niger, and President Philibert Tsiranana of Madagascar, are convinced that the Chinese are laying the groundwork to subvert Africa for an eventual takeover and intend to use it as a dumping ground for their surplus population. They urge Africans to have nothing to do with the Chinese. Others, like Julius Nyerere of Tanzania and President Modibo Keita of Mali, feel that the Chinese can be held at bay so long as they are carefully watched. They argue that an impoverished and struggling Africa cannot afford to spurn the foreign aid which China offers on very generous terms. Whoever is right, the fact remains that China ranks high among Africa's foreign policy concerns.

Prospects for the Future

If today in moderate Africa there is reason for hope and in revolutionary Africa cause for despair, it is because the issue which just a short time ago seemed to be settled—that Africa would and must develop by revolution rather than by evolution—no longer seems so certain. In many parts of the world today, the forces of revolution are in disarray. Far from consolidating their hold and spreading their influence to new areas, the revolutionaries have suffered severe setbacks. In Asia, China has been unable to cow India, and Sukarno's campaign of confrontation against Malaysia has failed, while he himself has been virtually stripped of power. In Africa, Ben Bella and Nkrumah have fallen, and with a vigorous opposition now organizing against Sékou Touré, his days also seem numbered. The government of Congo (Brazzaville) was recently confronted with a mutiny of its soldiers, angered over the presence and influence of Cuban mercenaries sent by Fidel Castro to help train President Alphonse Massamba-Débat's army.

Time is no longer working in favor of the revolutionary forces. Carefully planned but long-term economic development programs initiated years ago by some of the moderate leaders—over the dire warnings of the revolutionaries—have begun to bear fruit. Economic growth in the Ivory Coast over the last four years [1962-1966] has been an impressive 8 per cent, and per capita income has risen to $180 (as against $60 for Guinea); and comparable strides have been made in Nigeria, Gabon, and Cameroun. Meanwhile, Marxist programs launched with much fanfare six or seven years ago as shortcuts to a Socialist utopia have bogged down in a quagmire of shortages, red tape, and inefficient state management. The citizens of Africa's revolutionary countries are showing signs of disillusionment and even hostility toward leaders whose promises they believed in just a few short years ago.

It is unlikely that the contest beween the moderate and revolutionary forces in Africa will end in the complete triumph of one over the other. Nor would that be to Africa's advantage. To look at the contest through Western-tinted glasses and see it as a struggle of good against evil would be to misconstrue the political events of these last few years. It would also do grave injustice to the many positive contributions of the revolutionary forces to Africa's social development. The inner turbulence of the continent makes change quick and violent and events difficult to predict. As developments in Algeria and Ghana demonstrate, yesterday's revolutionaries may be tomorrow's moderates. And as Nigeria's sad plight shows, yesterday's model of stability may be tomorrow's center of chaos and anarchy.

The hope of most Africans is that the antogonisms which now rend their countries will one day disappear. When they do, they maintain, there will be neither moderates nor revolutionaries. It is then that the great ideal of African unity will be put to the test.

ZAMBIA DRAWS CLOSER TO EAST AFRICA [3]

Changes of emphasis in economic relationships between the countries of East and Central Africa in 1966 brought new hopes for the creation of a new and powerful black economic bloc.

While, individually, the three East African countries of Kenya, Tanzania and Uganda tended to weaken their economic ties with each other [a trend reversed in 1967—Ed.], collectively they laid increasing emphasis on forging new ties to the south—with Zambia.

During the year Zambia switched from being the most northerly territory in Southern Africa to the most southerly territory in East Africa.

Land-locked Zambia became even more so when Ian Smith's unilateral declaration of independence for Rhodesia threatened its lifeline through that country to Beira in Mozambique. New links were necessary, and Zambia looked northeasterly, to the Tanzanian ports of Mtwara and Dar es Salaam for outlets for its copper and other exports and as a supply source for imports and the 18,500 tons of oil it needs every month to keep its industry working.

Talks in Lusaka [Zambia's capital] and Dar es Salaam resulted in the signing of a $60 million contract to build an oil pipeline from Dar es Salaam to Ndola in the Zambian copper belt, an agreement to improve both the Tanzanian ports and Mtwara airport and the setting up of a joint transport company to run a nonstop 450-truck cargo haul service along the dusty Great North Road that links the two countries.

Hundreds of trucks are already trucking oil into Zambia and copper out.

[3] From "East Africa Draws Closer to Zambia." New York *Times.* p 58. Ja. 27, '67. © 1967 by The New York Times Company. Reprinted by permission.

That is not all. The economic boycott of Rhodesia, which once supplied 40 per cent of Zambia's $100 million . . . annual import requirements, has opened up large new markets to East African agriculture and industry.

Thus encouraged, the East African countries were instrumental in calling a twelve-nation conference in Addis Ababa in mid-year [1966] to take the first formal steps toward creating an Eastern African economic community.

Delegates from Kenya, Uganda, Tanzania, Ethiopia, the Sudan, Somalia, Malawi, Zambia, Madagascar, Mauritius, Rwanda and Burundi, which cover an area of more than 2.7 million square miles, and a potential consumer market of 75 million, agreed on Articles of Association.

These pledged them to promote coordinated development of their economies, to further the maximum possible interchange of goods and services, and to eliminate progressively customs and others barriers to trade expansion between them, as well as restrictions on current payment transactions and capital movements. . . .

East African countries were involved in discussions with the European Common Market during . . . [1966].

Talks Stalemated

Talks in Brussels in November between East African delegates and the EEC executive commission adjourned in stalemate, resulting from East Africa's refusal to grant specific tariff preferences to imports from the EEC in return for Common Market preference for East African goods. While the commission insisted on reciprocal preferences, the African countries contended that this arrangement would jeopardize their infant industries and harm its foreign trade, 75 per cent of which was outside the EEC countries. . . .

But East Africa's biggest economic disappointment during 1966 was the failure of Kenya, Tanzania and Uganda to resolve differences, which resulted in the breakup of the East African currency, the throwing up of interterritorial trade barriers and a general dissipation of the spirit of East African economic unity.

Each of the three nations issued its own currency during the year, Tanzania being the first to take the plunge, with the explanation that a national currency was necessary for its economic development. At the end of the year the three governments were studying the report of Professor Kjeld Philip, a United Nations Danish economic expert, who was asked to recommend on how the common market could be maintained and improved in the light of the currency breakup.

INSTABILITY IN THE CONGO [4]

1. No Rest for the Congo

[This article deals with the Democratic Republic of Congo (the former Belgian Congo) which has its capital at Kinshasa, formerly Leopoldville.—Ed.]

Few countries have had so many problems as the Congo in only seven years of existence. Most students of this part of Africa feel that the recurrent disorders stem from the disruptive independence period which first put the Congo in the headlines.

The Congo obtained its independence from a rather quick reversal of Belgian policy. On June 30, 1960, with almost no preparation, the Congo ended its colonial status. There were no Congolese officers in the Force Publique above the rank of sergeant or warrant officer. Some 1,200 Belgians ran this 25,000-man organization which was to become the national army or ANC. Moreover, the top five grades of the government administration contained less than 100 Congolese among 10,000 Belgians.

Until 1959 there were no plans for independence. Belgium had envisaged continued colonial status. The literacy rate was very high by African standards, but few Congolese children continued beyond the first four grades of primary school. Health conditions were very good, but there were only Belgian doctors. The proportion of Congolese working for wages was high for the region, but businesses were mostly owned and run by whites.

[4] From "No Rest for the Congo" and "Congolese Struggle to Regain Balance," two articles by Arthur H. House, assistant to the dean, the Fletcher School of Law and Diplomacy, Tufts University. *Christian Science Monitor* (Eastern edition). p 9. Ag. 19, p 5. O. 16, '67. Reprinted by permission from *The Christian Science Monitor*. © 1967 The Christian Science Publishing Society. All rights reserved.

Capabilities Damaged

Postindependence events and entry of the United Nations into the Congo in July 1960 to avoid a big-power clash have been vividly recorded. During the first two weeks of independence, army mutiny against the remaining white officers and the central government and a mass flight of technicians inflicted immense damage on the operating capabilities of the country. The 1,200 white officers left the army. Except for Katanga Province (which under Moise Tshombe seceded almost immediately after the Congo became independent) there were only about 800 technicians left from the 10,000 on duty at the time of independence.

The political history of the Congo since 1960 reflects the wrenching effects of the virtually complete elimination of the colonial elite and the resulting vacuum. There are four main reasons for the consequent disruption of the country:

Internal weakness. This has been and continues to be one of the most important reasons for unrest.

Immense potential wealth. Eighty per cent of the world's industrial diamonds come from the Congo. There are large copper, tin, and cobalt ore deposits and extensive facilities to mine them. An unusual feature of the Congo is the large percentage of wage earners outside the subsistence sector of the economy. This supply of salaried workers in commerce, manufacturing, and services is adaptable to new industries and capable of supplying goods and services to other African states.

Strategic location. The Congo lies between the white-ruled minority governments of southern Africa and black Africa to the north. In size it is as large as the United States east of the Mississippi. It borders on ten other states and is the heart of Equatorial Africa.

Foreign intervention. This follows from the previous reasons. With the internal weakness of the Congo, the wealth scattered close to its borders, and an encirclement of generally weak neighbors, foreign nations and organized outsiders continue to intervene in various ways to support their own interests and elements other than the central government.

The lack of adequate, trained personnel lies at the root of the problem. For the Congo, as for all developing nations, a prime necessity is an effective, responsible, and disciplined army both for defense and for internal security. Secondly, it needs civil technicians from mechanics and accountants to teachers, doctors, and engineers.

The presence of UN troops from July 1960 until June 1964 partially alleviated this lack. However, the "blue helmets" were in the Congo to prevent external involvement. They did not retrain the ANC or instruct officers; nor could they be counted on to maintain internal security if such action entailed involvement in domestic affairs.

So, at the end of 1962 the Secretary-General of the United Nations invited bilateral agreements to give military aid to the Congo. Diverse and limited assistance programs have been, at various times, of some help. Israel has helped to instruct paratroopers (including the Congolese president, General Joseph Mobutu). Italy and Belgium have trained pilots and army officers respectively. The United States gave equipment and advice through the United Nations until 1962, and has continued assistance until the present through bilateral accords.

Such piecemeal programs have produced some fine officers and improved certain parts of the army. But the ANC has never received the complete overhaul it needs.

In 1960, as well as moving in troops, the United Nations recruited over one thousand civilian technicians to form the largest technical-assistance team ever assembled by the organization. It was extremely difficult to find French-speaking people to fill the huge gap left by Belgian withdrawal. But a complete collapse was averted in the second half of 1960, and skeleton holding-operations kept essential services intact. These international technicians, together with the rapidly promoted Congolese, although thrown into jobs way above their training, staved off what could have been an enormous disaster.

Experts Cut Back

The United States paid a good deal of the costs of this civilian operation—and still does. Training programs were established and now the Congolese themselves are assuming more responsibilities each year. About 450 UN experts are still in the Congo; but this number will be severely reduced next year [1968].

The difference between the civilian and military crises is significant.

The UN technicians have maintained an extraordinary program on an emergency basis. With considerable use of American counterpart funds, the technical training institutes are turning out qualified personnel to take over when the international personnel withdraws.

The military situation is different. The ANC has regained some discipline from the days of mutinies and chaos immediately following independence. Yet despite this the force is not yet considered a viable, self-sufficient security force. The two main inadequacies are equipment and personnel.

Three examples demonstrate this:

1. The Katanga secession from July 1960 to the end of 1962. The secession was caused and supported by foreign elements in the Congo. It was ended by foreign forces, namely United Nations troops aided by American transport and equipment.

2. The rebellion of 1964 and 1965. Several indigenous rebellions grew into "the 1964-65 rebellion" as a result of lack of security, disruption of normal economic activity, and almost complete neglect for provincial affairs since the breakdown following independence. This became a serious threat when supported by the Chinese Communists and when Soviet, Czech, and Chinese arms were supplied to the rebels through certain neighboring nations. It was ended by reinforcing the ANC with foreign mercenaries and with Belgian and American equipment and assistance.

3. The latest insurrection of foreign mercenaries. It appears that the mercenaries are spearheading an effort organized from outside the Congo. Reports from Brussels at the beginning of July indicated

that there was an unusual amount of activity among former mercenaries. Reports from Rwanda say that the Katangese gendarmes and mercenaries who recaptured Bukavu were wearing new uniforms and carrying automatic weapons. The insurrection appears to be directly linked with the kidnaping of former Prime Minister Moise Tshombe.

The ANC gained stature at first by driving the mercenaries out of Bukavu. The Congo at that time requested from the United States and received three transport planes manned by paratroopers of the United States 82d Airborne Division. However, the more recent defeats inflicted upon the ANC by the approximately two hundred mercenaries and their several hundred Katanga gendarmes —they reoccupied Bukavu August 8 [1967]—have once again raised doubts about the ANC's capabilities. The ANC's own need for mercenaries and its temporary borrowing of American planes and paratroopers reflect the gaps which still exist in its effectiveness.

The current episode of mercenary activity somewhat clouds the issue as to who the mercenaries are and whose side they are on.

The first mercenaries were former metropolitan Belgian officers and other recruits who staffed the Katanga army when Katanga under Moise Tshombe seceded from the Congo in July 1960. They were later joined by some anti-Gaullist French, many of them Algerian veterans, who operated as a separate unit in Katanga. These Europeans, and some others in the Bakwanga area, stayed until Katanga's secession was ended by the UN in 1962.

Rebellion Suppressed

Some of these mercenaries fled to Angola, some withdrew to more remote parts of Katanga, and some just disappeared. In general they remained loyal to Mr. Tshombe. In fact his power base with such mercenaries and their willingness to fight for him when the rebellion broke out in 1964 were factors which helped Mr. Tshombe to become prime minister of the Congo after the withdrawal of UN forces.

These colorful adventurers, divided into English-speaking and French-speaking units, were employed this time by the Congo government itself—Moise Tshombe. They drew world attention for their success in turning the tide and eventually suppressing the 1964-65 rebellion. Before this second group of mercenaries was brought together many thought the Congo would be lost. Even so, the use of mercenaries, especially South Africans, drew criticism from other African nations.

The third group of mercenaries, those currently in the news, are really carryovers from the 1964-65 rebellion. When President Mobutu came to power on November 24, 1965, the rebellion was largely under control although sporadic outbursts and control operations still continued, and every so often some men would be lost. So President Mobutu disbanded the English-speaking battalion and decorated its leader, "Mad Mike" Hoare of South Africa. But he retained the French-speaking sixth battalion under Colonel Robert Denard, a Frenchman, with about 150 men.

In April [1967] this correspondent heard Colonel Denard reaffirm his allegiance to General Mobutu. But the fighting role of his mercenaries appeared then to be fading away. He contemplated —reluctantly—adding more Congolese to his numbers and using the enlarged battalion to assist in economic development of the ravaged northeast Congo.

However, it appears that someone else made a more attractive offer for the use of his men, even though they were already being paid, his officers told me, about $800 a month in hard currency. After this, it is unlikely that any Congo government will rely again on mercenaries.

American Policy

The United States has pursued a consistent policy toward the Congo's civilian technician gap. The United Nations operational and advisory personnel are largely paid for with American funds.

The needs are still vast; the devastation and disorder of the 1964-65 rebellion created a great need for continued training of Congolese. Agriculture has yet to recover. The disengagement of the United Nations technicians is causing strain; only time will show if the trainees are able to assume positions requiring considerable expertise and experience. Little has been done to ameliorate the conditions which originally caused the 1964-65 rebellion. Many observers consider future difficulties probable.

American military policy has not been so consistent. American assistance has been in three forms: a military mission is in the Congo for advice to the ANC and for normal military relations; use of equipment is provided in emergencies, such as the C-130 transport planes used . . . [in July 1967] and during the last rebellion; finally, American operational fighting soldiers have been used on occasion since 1960.

The mission is a routine institution. The requests for equipment in emergencies are quite normal and logical. Many other nations depend on the United States for military equipment in times of crisis. Such temporary arrangements are designed to prevent indiscriminate use of military equipment, prevent arms races, and lessen the military expenses of nations trying to develop. It is a credit to the American political and military field personnel that such requests often come to this nation rather than to Communist-bloc nations.

The use of American fighting personnel and condoning the use of mercenaries is considered by many to be less commendable. Ever since independence the Congo has had to rely on foreign personnel, either in an emergency capacity as in the Belgian-American airdrop on Stanleyville in 1964 or in the form of mercenaries.

The United States has become committed to preserving the unity and territorial integrity of the Congo. But it has only allocated short-term instruments to assure the country's internal security. Since independence the United States has maintained the major embassy in the Congo, and the Congo mission has been the largest American mission in Africa. It has been very competently staffed and has provided the bulk of assistance toward the formation of a stable, progressive government. . . . On May 17, 1967, Under Secretary of State Nicholas deB. Katzenbach assured the Congo of the "support of the Government and people of the United States of America, as you progress in unity toward increased stability and prosperity."

Yet the United States has never relieved the Congo of the need to rely in one way or another on foreign military personnel. The absence of qualified, trained personnel in the armed forces can be as disruptive as has been reliance on foreign personnel. The proficiency of a few professionally trained Congolese officers demonstrates the advantages a complete retraining of the ANC could bring. . . .

2. *Congolese Struggle to Regain Balance*

The current regime under President Mobutu has been able to profit from reinforcement of nationalist aspirations. His confident handling of the Union Minière crisis and the subsequent announcement that "the Congo of Papa is dead" brought a good deal of local and external African support.

He also seems to be finally ridding the Congo of the last mercenaries who previously provided the striking force in the northeast regions. He has nationalized the insurance companies.

His immediate advisers now are predominantly Congolese. His counsel on economic affairs comes from a young but bright economist named Jacques Bongoma who was educated at Louvain and the London School of Economics.

The daily news is preceded by dramatic strains of Beethoven's Fifth Symphony followed by nationalist exhortations to unity and strength.

Yet unity and strength, or state preservation, and Africanization must be looked upon as separate issues in the near future. President Mobutu will need skilled personnel faster than the Congo is producing them.

The magnitude of deterioration is depressing. Vast areas have been without contact with the central government, ravaged by violence, or simply neglected so that they have sunk into subsistence.

Foreign technicians are needed to run the mining complex. Without the mercenaries and in light of their alarming power to control sections of the country, the weakness of the army is apparent. And the UN feels compelled to phase down its assistance.

The task ahead resembles reconquest. But the Mobutu government seems to have considerable support at this time; it may now be in a position to tackle it.

Normalcy in the Congo means that the problems themselves rather than merely their symptoms can receive attention.

RACE WAR IN NEIGHBORING SUDAN [5]

Tens of thousands killed . . . hundreds of thousands homeless—

These are not casualty figures of a natural disaster but of a little-noticed racial war in the deep south of the Sudan that has plagued this country for four years.

Although the war has dropped off in intensity lately, it is still bringing death and devastation to an area bigger than the state of Texas.

Cause of the fighting is an attempt by the national government to "integrate" a black, non-Arab, non-Moslem minority of southerners into a country ruled by a powerful majority of Arab Moslems. The southerners refuse to be integrated. They would like independence—a separate state for the tribes who live in the provinces of the deep south.

The peoples of the two regions are quite different. The vast majority of southerners are Hamitic types—tall, lean, flat-nosed and very black. Most are pagan, but nearly half a million have been converted to Christianity.

Northerners regard themselves as superior and more civilized. They are Moslems. Skin color ranges from light tan to very dark. All of them speak Arabic, and consider themselves to be of the Arab world.

Roots of trouble between the two groups go back many years, but the situation began to turn ugly in 1963 when it became evident that the Sudan government was not going to relent in its drive for "unity" through which northerners would eventually dominate the south.

[5] "Africa's 'Hidden' Race War." Reprinted from *U.S. News & World Report*. 63:56. O. 23, '67.

Groups of southern guerrillas, armed with everything from spears to Chinese automatic weapons, began hit-and-run attacks against troops of the Sudanese army.

Schools and hospitals in the area closed down. Teachers and doctors—most of them northerners—fled. Many of them had been assaulted by their students.

Three hundred foreign missionaries, accused of supporting the rebels, were expelled from the country.

Sudanese government forces then began massive reprisals against rebel areas. Whole villages were burned, tribesmen flogged or killed. Villagers by the tens of thousands fled into the bush.

On one wild night, in the provincial capital of Juba, Sudanese troops killed nearly 1,400 men, women and children to avenge the death of a sergeant.

No one knows how many have died in the Sudanese war. Estimates range from 10,000 to 500,000. A figure of 50,000 is probably closest to being accurate.

The world has learned relatively little about the war in the south because few newsmen are allowed by officials to visit the area.

From fragments of information that find their way to Khartoum, however, it is possible to piece together a fair idea of the situation in the south.

Guerrillas in the Countryside

The towns are garrisoned and tightly controlled by the Sudanese army, but it doesn't control the countryside. There, guerrillas lay ambushes for supply trucks and jeeps. Few officials leave their headquarters, because making a visit to their "district" requires the mounting of a small military expedition for their protection.

The level of guerrilla activity has dropped off now because the guerrillas are running short of arms and ammunition. Their supplies from neighboring countries have been choked off.

But southern resistance goes on. Neither side shows any sign of giving in.

Northerners say they will not even discuss the possibility of a settlement until, in the words of one, "we have restored order first." On the other hand, a rebel leader told a foreigner recently: "The

Arabs have committed so many unprovoked atrocities that our people will no longer accept anything but independence."

In the meantime, the southern Sudan is slipping backward.

For four years, there have been no schools or hospitals operating.

Christian churches stand empty because the missionaries are gone and most of the African clergymen have disappeared into the bush. Illiteracy and ill health are increasing.

The way things are going now, there is every prospect that racial conflict in Sudan's deep south will continue, adding an increasingly heavy burden of tragedy to an already unhappy land.

FUTURE PROSPECTS—AN AMERICAN VIEW [6]

In the Congo there is a wise proverb: "Let him speak who has seen with his eyes."

It is so with this great continent. In the United States one can imagine Africa from the stereotypes generated by films and zoos and masks in museums. One can hear about Africa from a growing number of Americans with ties here. One can read about Africa from a swelling number of books. But none of this data can produce more than a Mercator projection. None of it can convey the vitality of Africa, the equal vitality of old villages and new cities. None of it can convey the diversity and spirit of your people. I can say this because, heeding the proverb, I have come to see with my own eyes. . . .

It has been observed that travelers are justified in describing what they have seen and need not rise to generalization. I might be greatly tempted to take that observation to heart, for we have seen magnificent things. Yet it is impossible to settle for mere description. The contrasts are still more startling than the sights.

In West Africa we saw the sun set on an uninhabited rain forest beach just as it might have ten centuries ago. But only a few miles away, in Dakar, we saw a spectacular urban renewal project housing sixty thousand.

[6] From "America and Africa, the New World and the Newer World," address delivered at Haile Selassie I University in Addis Ababa, Ethiopia, May 26, 1967, by Nicholas deB. Katzenbach, United States Under Secretary of State. Text from *Department of State Bulletin.* 56:954-9. Je. 26, '67.

In Zambia we saw men pulling wooden carts to market. But only a few miles away we saw giant cargo planes unloading barrels of oil and taking on tons of copper ingots, all within twelve minutes.

In Ghana we saw a village woman in a red loincloth cooking over an open fire. But only a few yards away we saw energy pouring out of the giant orange penstocks of the Volta River Dam.

We have seen, in short, the old Africa and the new.

Power of Revolutionary Change

If the changes that are taking place are far reaching, they are not unique to this continent. The whole world feels the power of revolutionary change. One level is external: the change in international relations impelled by the headlong technological advances of the past few decades. A second level is internal: the attempts by new nations to find appropriate institutions and responses to meet the needs of their peoples.

Change is all about us, and yet w. are only dimly aware of the forces that it unleashes. The giant Volta River Dam at Akosombo means power, industry, and economic strength. But consider the problems that have come with it:

—The vast reservoir behind the dam has displaced thousands of families.

—After generations of fishing in a swift river, those who remain must now learn to catch lake fish.

—Medical specialists brood about which new diseases will be bred in the now still water.

On a larger scale, we send men into space. We communicate instantaneously with the most distant nations by satellites. His Imperial Majesty [Haile Selassie, Emperor of Ethiopia] this year has twice flown to North America more easily than he traveled to the provinces not many years ago. Yet we are still trying to find a way to bring something so fundamental as human dignity and self-determination to the Africans in the southern part of this continent.

This is a cause in which we stand with you, conscience to conscience. Not for economic gain, not for political advantage, not for cosmetic appearance, but because we share the certainty once expressed by President [of Zambia Kenneth] Kaunda: "We shall win because we are right."

Parallels in Development

As striking as these contrasts in change may be, I find myself impressed by some striking parallels between the new world of America and the newer world of Africa.

I do not mean America of the moment, for that is a deceptive model. First, America may be wealthy, America may be advanced, America may be a world power, but America also is troubled by internal problems. Like Africa, like other parts of the world, my country encompasses a great underdeveloped country, an underdeveloped America of citizens who are poor, who often are ignorant, and who for too long have been ignored. President Johnson and his administration have made the uplifting of these people a prime domestic goal, but that goal cannot soon be achieved.

Second, America of today is a deceptive model precisely because it is the developed America of today. Our concern, our devoted concern here, is the Africa of tomorrow.

What do I mean, then, by striking parallels between America and Africa? I mean parallels in development—the factors in the growth of my country which have relevance to the growth of the new nations of your continent.

Let me focus on three of these factors.

The first is education, and I would like to begin by reading you a passage I find unusually descriptive:

. . . what sphere of patriotic exertion is left open for the lover of his country, but the sphere of improving the rising generation through the instrumentality of a more perfect and efficient system for their education?

We call our fathers patriots, because they loved their country and made sacrifices for its welfare. But what was their country? A vast tract of wilderness territory did not constitute it. It was not unconscious, insentient plains, or rivers, or mountains, however beautifully and majestically they might spread, or flow, or shine, beneath the canopy of heaven. Their country was chiefly their descendants, the human beings who were to throng these vast domains, the sentient, conscious natures which were to live here, and living, to enjoy or suffer.

These words were written in 1842 by Horace Mann, an American and a leading exponent of public education. They have relevance to Africa now. Efforts like his were successful. The United States initiated widespread free public education. Was it merely coincidence that my country's mushrooming rush to industrial power began approximately fifteen years later?

The importance Africa places on education is evident from statistics. Of fifty-three African universities, thirty have been created since 1952 and eleven since 1961. The number of all students on this continent has nearly tripled in fifteen years, from 9 million in 1950 to 27 million today. The number of university students has gone from 70,000 in 1950 to more than 250,000.

Yet it is impossible to take too much cheer from such statistics, for there are other figures which suggest the enormity of the job ahead. University enrollment may be 180,000 greater than it was fifteen years ago. Yet at the same time, the number of university-aged Africans has increased by 3 million in just the past five years.

Building a Transportation Network

A second parallel between developing Africa and America when it was developing is transportation.

America began as a nation of 4 million, largely settled, like many of your countries, on the coastal fringe of a vast land containing vast mineral and agricultural treasure.

Unlocking that wilderness was an immediate goal. Even before the steam engine had been invented, we had completed what was then a national road. When the railroad did come, it became an object of high priority.

In 1830 America had twenty-three miles of railroads. Twenty-five years later there were eighteen thousand miles of railroads. Five years after that, in 1860, there were thirty thousand miles.

I believe it is fair to say that from 1840 until the turn of the century transportation—the railroad—was the key to American success.

In 1869 came an historic date that symbolizes much of our past and your future—the completion of a transcontinental railroad line—a line that tied a vast nation together; a line that allowed ore, wheat, and timber to be taken out; a line that allowed men to come in.

"The railroad," an American historian has written, "tied the North and West into one massive free economy. It did much more. It tied business to politics and both to the life of the individual in a way unknown in America before."

What these words say about America seems to me to have great force on this continent.

The parallel with present-day Africa is indeed striking. The new nations of this continent require circulatory lifeblood, allowing the transport of your natural wealth and the ready infusion of human resources to help develop it.

In the Africa of the late twentieth century, transportation might well center on highways, or even air routes, rather than railroads. But the principle—and the potential—are the same.

Agriculture and Natural Resources

Finally, let me turn to agriculture and natural resources. When America was settled, there were vast expanses of fertile but inaccessible land. There were hidden treasures in minerals. It was the railroad that opened up those riches to development. As transportation improved young America could go beyond farming for subsistence and become a source of food for others; our Midwest was built on a foundation of wheat for the world.

The fertility provided by nature and the accessibility provided by technology were supported by another factor: extensive Government-private cooperation to improve both the production and the lives of our farm population.

One great advance was an act of Congress of 1862 providing for colleges to promote knowledge of "agriculture and mechanic arts." In short order, such institutions were established in almost every eligible state.

These did more than train young men and women in needed skills. Through extension centers, they went out to the people. Ultimately, through resident agents in each county, they reached out to virtually every part of our agricultural areas. These county agents brought practical advice as well as technical and scientific information—not only to farmers but also to their wives and families.

The parallels of mineral and agricultural potential in this continent are plain. There is great need for information, tutelage, and advice at the village level. There is a need at least as great for instruction and assistance in marketing and distribution. Here in Ethiopia, the Agricultural High School at Jimma and the College of Agriculture at Alemaya are pioneering efforts on a fruitful frontier. For Africa could become an agricultural heartland for the world, given your unlimited potential for production. That is a potential for more than one-crop economies, for a wide diversity of crops, some with industrial applicability. And it is a potential for more than agricultural production, for it could readily lead to the development of the food-processing industry.

However appropriate these parallels may be, there is a basic defect in each of them: America was able to devise these answers to development alone and at its own pace for two reasons—reasons which make it possible for Americans to be thankful that our Thirteen Colonies won their independence in a simpler day.

One of these reasons is that we came to independence at a time when it was possible for us to be truly independent—to hold ourselves aloof from the rest of the world.

Though we were impoverished, we were left alone to build a nation and find our destiny. For decades, we found a watchword in Washington's farewell address: "It is our true policy to steer clear of permanent alliances with any portion of the foreign world."

For us, nonalignment was an easy task.

The second reason is that, unlike some thirty new African nations, we became independent in a time when technological change was slow and slight.

Our arms were rudimentary, but they fired as well—sometimes better—than the naval cannon and muskets of imperial Britain.

Our economy was simple, but then so was that of every country, in a time when concepts like gross national product were a century away from definition.

And our industry was primitive, for there was no other sort of industry. It was conducted on spinning wheels and blacksmiths' anvils. The world had not yet even dreamed of megatons or mega-watts, aluminum smelters, or titanium airplanes.

In short, newly independent America had time—time to explore itself, time to educate itself, time to learn new vocabularies and new technologies as they were devised.

By contrast, the new nations of Africa have been called to the main stage immediately—to go from the spear to the slide rule, from disunited tribes to the United Nations virtually in months.

Need for Skilled and Educated Africans

Can this transition be made with the speed which the influential young men and women of Africa believe necessary?

That is not a question for an outsider to answer. It is a central question in virtually every new African nation. Their answers undoubtedly will vary. I would suggest, however, that there are two irreducible factors to which we must reconcile ourselves, factors which must limit the telescoping of time on this continent.

The first of these factors is human capabilities. The education of intelligent men and women in complex skills can be improved in quality. It can be enlarged in quantity. But no amount of good motives, nor wealth, nor wisdom can, without the passage of time, produce the pool of skilled and educated African men and women who are required to manage the affairs and fuel the spirit of a modern nation.

You here in this eminent institution will be frontiersmen in that effort. But not until your numbers swell—as surely they will—can this country and your sister countries on this continent find the manpower with which to generate widespread growth.

Emphasis on Cooperative Development

The second factor to which I believe we must reconcile ourselves follows the first. It is suggested occasionally that the development time gap could be overcome if only developed nations like the United States would more fully meet responsibilities of assistance to the underdeveloped world.

As a son of a free country and as a friend of Africa, I am unable to accept this case. It is theoretically possible for major industrial powers to send huge sums and corps of technicians to build and operate factories or transportation systems or railroads. And by doing so they would help build nations in Africa. But they would not be African nations in Africa. As we oppose neocolonialism, so should we oppose such a false solution.

President Johnson has observed accurately that development cannot be exported. And President [of Tanzania Julius K.] Nyerere has said of his people, they "recognize that the task of economic development is a long and heavy one . . . our people do not believe that it is better to be a wealthy slave than a poor free man."

By no means do I wish to suggest that African nations can avoid losing their independence only by refusing outside assistance. Nor do I wish to suggest that already developed nations should not assist those parts of humanity who are coming late to political manhood. What I do believe is that, in the interests both of developed and developing nations, developmental assistance must be carefully offered—and it must be carefully received.

In his speech on Africa a year ago, President Johnson outlined a policy for such assistance, noting that:

The world has now reached a stage where some of the most effective means of economic growth can best be achieved in large units commanding large resources and large markets. Most nation-states are too small, when acting alone, to assure the welfare of all of their people.

This is the principle which underlies our present policy of aid for Africa—cooperation among donors and cooperation among recipients.

This is not a new philosophy for us. Nearly a third of the aid we have provided in the past has been for projects benefiting not merely one country but several.

We are assisting river development in the Senegal River, Niger River, and Lake Chad basins. We are working with an organization of fourteen Central African nations to combat measles, smallpox, rinderpest, and bovine pneumonia. In this decade Ethiopia and four other African countries have combined, with American and British support, to form the Desert Locust Control Authority, whose efforts have been completely successful. We have helped to establish advanced education institutions, like the regional heavy equipment training center in Togo.

Neither is such a cooperative policy new in the relations of other countries. The nations of Western Europe have made striking progress in the past decade toward a common market. The leaders of Latin America have just pledged themselves to work toward a similar goal.

The aim of our cooperative policy is simple: maximum benefit for all the new nations of Africa. We do not seek to dictate development priorities to recipient countries. The fact is that virtually every nation has the same developmental priorities to begin with—the same sort of priorities which I described as paralleling the experience of my country—education, transportation, and agricultural and natural-resource development.

Nor is it our aim to require rigid cooperative groupings. The new nations of Africa have varying links to each other. River development may run north and south; a railroad may benefit two nations; a public health program may involve fourteen.

We shall look with particular interest for programs organized by existing multilateral organizations: the World Bank, the African Development Bank, ECA [Economic Commission for Africa], and the OAU. At the same time, we will welcome project proposals devised directly by the participating countries. Indeed, the competition among them may well serve as a spur and thus itself help bring the economies of scale to African development.

Impulse Toward African Unity

Even beyond flexibility, beyond economies of scale, beyond the more beneficial use of developmental assistance, our new emphasis on cooperation among donors and cooperation among recipients can have another result, a result which may, in the end, be the most important of all. It can serve as an additional impulse toward African unity.

In my various conversations across this continent I have found unity a goal that is widely shared and a goal that is particularly prized by young people. They see their young countries struggling against the arbitrary divisions inflicted by the colonial period—divisions created by inherited boundaries, divisions created by the imposition of different Western languages, divisions created by different levels of colonial development.

It is this aspect of cooperative development that is to me the most hopeful and the most exciting. For if it is conducted among groupings established by the recipient countries themselves, it seems to me that it can be an important force toward the eventual conquest of those arbitrary divisions.

We believe, in short, that this policy of coordination among donors and cooperation among recipients is sound. We hope it will be successful. But even if it succeeds beyond our wildest expectations, it can only hasten—and not bring about—the emergence of Africa as a community of strong and confident nations, able and willing to make their contribution to the welfare of their people and of the world.

And that work, that very difficult and patient and inspired and patriotic work, must be yours. The present leaders of Africa have begun that work with wisdom and courage. It will be in your lifetimes—and indeed because of your lifetimes—that this work will come to fruition, that the land, and the people who animate the land, and the spirit that animates your people, will make their mighty contribution to the world.

I think of the words of President [of Senegal Léopold S.] Senghor, describing the spirit Africa can give to the world:

> For who would teach rhythm to a dead world of machines and guns?
> Who would give the cry of joy to wake the dead and the bereaved at the dawn?
> Say, who would give back the memory of life to the man whose hopes are smashed?

I see, much more clearly now, what he means. Africa will not be easily mastered. One has only to see the struggle of wresting crops from difficult soil and hostile climate to know that it has taken people of character to make something of the land. It has taken courage, tenacity, humor, creativity—in short, spirit.

What has impressed me, then, about Africa is not so much its vastness, nor its resource potential, nor its beauty, but its people.

The foundation of Africa is the spirit of its people.

Africa is on the move. I knew that before I came. Now I believe it.

BIBLIOGRAPHY

An asterisk (*) preceding a reference indicates that the article or a part of it has been reprinted in this book.

Books, Pamphlets, and Documents

Apter, D. E. Political kingdom in Uganda. Princeton University Press. Princeton, N.J. '67.

Ashby, Eric. African universities and western tradition. Harvard University Press. Cambridge, Mass. '64.

Bienen, Henry. Tanzania: party transformation and economic development. Princeton University Press. Princeton, N.J. '67.

Boyd, Andrew and Van Rensburg, Patrick. Atlas of African affairs. Praeger. New York. '65.

Brzezinski, Z. K. ed. Africa and the Communist world. Stanford University Press. Stanford, Calif. '63.

Carter, G. M. ed. Politics in Africa: 7 cases. Harcourt. New York. '66.

Chilcote, R. H. Portuguese Africa. Prentice-Hall. Englewood Cliffs, N.J. '67.

Coleman, J. S. and Rosberg, C. G. Jr. eds. Political parties and national integration in tropical Africa. University of California Press. Berkeley. '64.

Cooley, J. K. East wind over Africa: Red China's African offensive. Walker. New York. '65.

Council on World Tensions. Africa: progress through cooperation; ed. by John Karefa-Smart. Dodd. New York. '66.

Cowan, L. G. Dilemmas of African independence. Walker. New York. '64.

Cowan, L. G. and others, eds. Education and nation-building in Africa. Praeger. New York. '65.

Cox, Richard. Kenyatta's country. Praeger. New York. '65.
Review. Saturday Review. 49:37-8+. Jl. 9, '66. Charles Miller.

Dostert, P. E. and Post, E. T. Africa 1966. Stryker-Post Publications. Washington, D.C. '66.

*Du Bois, V. D. African ferment: 1966. (West Africa Series. v 9) American Universities Field Staff. Reports Service. 366 Madison Ave. New York 10017. '66.

Dumont, René. False start in Africa; tr. by P. N. Ott. Praeger. New York. '66.

Emerson, Rupert. Africa and United States policy. Prentice-Hall. Englewood Cliffs, N.J. '67.

Emerson, Rupert and Kilson, Martin, eds. Political awakening of Africa. Prentice-Hall. Englewood Cliffs, N.J. '65.

Ferkiss, V. C. Africa's search for identity. Meridian. Cleveland. '67.

*First National City Bank. Foreign Information Service. East and Central Africa—a survey of six developing countries. The Bank. 399 Park Ave. New York 10022. '66.
    Copies of this report are no longer available.

*Fordham, Paul. Geography of African affairs. Penguin. Baltimore. '65.

Geiger, Theodore and Armstrong, Winifred. Development of African private enterprise. National Planning Association. 1606 New Hampshire Ave. N.W. Washington, D.C. 20009. '64.

Ginzberg, Eli and Smith, H. A. Manpower strategy for developing countries: lessons from Ethiopia. Columbia University Press. New York. '67.

Goldschmidt, Walter, ed. United States and Africa. Praeger (for the American Assembly). New York. '63.

Gower, L. C. B. Independent Africa: the challenge to the legal profession. Harvard University Press. Cambridge, Mass. '66.

Greenfield, R. D. Ethiopia: a new political history. Praeger. New York. '65.
    Review. Nation. 202:132-4. Ja. 31, '66.

Hance, W. A. African economic development. Praeger (for the Council on Foreign Relations). New York. '67.

Hance, W. A. Geography of modern Africa. Columbia University Press. New York. '64.

Hapgood, David. Africa: from independence to tomorrow. Atheneum. New York. '65.

Hatch, J. C. History of postwar Africa. Praeger. New York. '65.

Henderson, K. D. D. Sudan Republic. Praeger. New York. '65.

Hughes, A. J. East Africa: the search for unity—Kenya, Tanganyika, Uganda, and Zanzibar. Penguin. Baltimore. '64.

Ingham, Kenneth. History of East Africa. Praeger. New York. '67.

International Bank for Reconstruction and Development. Economic development of Kenya. Johns Hopkins Press. Baltimore. '63.

Kenyatta, Jomo. Facing Mount Kenya. Vintage. New York. '62.

Legum, Colin. Pan-Africanism: a short political guide. Praeger. New York. '65.

Levitt, Leonard. African season. Simon & Schuster. New York. '67.
    Excerpt entitled: How do you like Africa, young man; is it like New York? *Harper's Magazine.* 234:82-8. Ja. '67.

Lewis, I. M. Modern history of Somaliland. Praeger. New York. '65.

Listowel, Judith. Making of Tanganyika. British Book Centre. New York. '66.

Little, I. M. D. Aid to Africa. Macmillan. New York. '64.

Lloyd, P. C. Africa in social change. Penguin. Baltimore. '67.

Lofchie, M. F. Zanzibar: background to revolution. Princeton University Press. Princeton, N.J. '65.

MacDonald, Alexander. Tanzania: young nation in a hurry. Hawthorn. New York. '66.

McKay, Vernon, ed. African diplomacy: studies in the determinants of foreign policy. Praeger. New York. '66.

Masland, J. W. Educational development in Africa: the role of United States assistance. (Occasional Report. no 4) Education and World Affairs. New York. '67.

Mazrui, A. A. Towards a Pax Africana: a study of ideology and ambition. University of Chicago Press. Chicago. '67.

Mezu, S. O. ed. Philosophy of pan-Africanism. Georgetown University Press. Washington, D.C. '65.

Miller, J. D. B. Politics of the third world. Oxford University Press. New York. '67.

Nye, J. S. Jr. Pan-Africanism and East African integration. Harvard University Press. Cambridge, Mass. '65.

Oliver, Roland and Fage, J. D. Short history of Africa. Penguin. Baltimore. '62.

Quigg, P. W. ed. Africa: a Foreign Affairs reader. Praeger. New York. '64.

*Rivkin, Arnold. New states of Africa. (Headline Series. no 183) Foreign Policy Association. 345 E. 46th St. New York 10017. '67.

*Rosberg, C. G. Jr. (with Aaron Segal). An East African federation. (International Conciliation. no 543) Carnegie Endowment for International Peace. United Nations Plaza at 46th St. New York 10017. '63.

Rosberg, C. G. Jr. and Nottingham, J. C. Myth of Mau Mau: nationalism in Kenya. Praeger. New York. '66.

    Review. New Republic. 156:34-5. F. 25, '67. Martin Lowenkopf.

Rotberg, R. I. Political history of tropical Africa. Harcourt. New York. '65.

Spiro, H. J. ed. Patterns of African development—5 comparisons. Prentice-Hall. Englewood Cliffs, N.J. '67.

Taylor, J. C. Political development of Tanganyika. Stanford University Press. Stanford, Calif. '63.

Taylor, Sidney, ed. New Africans. Reuters guide to the contemporary history of emergent Africa and its leaders. Putnam. New York. '67.

Thiam, Doudou. Foreign policy of African states. Praeger. New York. '65.

Touval, Saadia. Somali nationalism: international politics and the drive for unity in the Horn of Africa. Harvard University Press. Cambridge, Mass. '63.

Turnbull, C. M. Lonely African. Simon & Schuster. New York. '62.

Ullendorff, Edward. Ethiopians: an introduction to country and people. Oxford University Press. New York. '65.

United States. Department of State. Office of Media Services. United States and Africa. (Publication 7710. African series 40) Supt. of Docs. Washington, D.C. 20402. '64.

Wallerstein, I. M. Africa: the politics of independence. Vintage. New York. '61.

Wallerstein, I. M. Africa: the politics of unity. Random House. New York. '67.

Wallerstein, I. M. ed. Social change, the colonial situation. Wiley. New York. '66.

Zartman, I. W. International relations in the New Africa. Prentice-Hall. Englewood Cliffs, N.J. '66.

PERIODICALS

Africa Report. 12:5-13. F. '67. Rhodesia since UDI. L. W. Bowman.

Africa Report. 12:14-20. F. '67. Rhodesia's African majority. Davis M'Gabe

*Africa Report. 12:8-10. Mr. '67. Meaning of Arusha. Martin Lowenkopf.

Africa Report. 12:11-13. Mr. '67. Policy of self-reliance; excerpts from Part III of the Arusha Declaration of February 5, 1967.

Africa Report. 12:14-20+. Mr. '67. Escape from stagnation. Tom Mboya.

Africa Report. 12:46-50. Mr. '67. After the Lagos agreement. Arnold Rivkin.

Africa Report. 12:37-8+. Ap. '67. Prospects in the Horn. I. M. Lewis.

Africa Report. 12:46-50. Ap. '67. Politics of land in East Africa. Aaron Segal.

Africa Report. 12:20-3+. Je. '67. Economic cooperation in Africa. A. M. Stillman.

Africa Report. 12:55-8. Je. '67. Domino theory of the Rhodesian lobby. Vernon McKay.

Africa Report. 12:59-61. Je '67. Language and politics in East Africa. A. A. Mazrui.

Africa Report. 12:72-9. Je. '67. Education for self-reliance; an African Report supplement. J. K. Nyerere.

Africa Report. 12:12-15. O. '67. Congo-Kinshasa situation report. M. C. Young.

Africa Report. 12:58-61. O. '67. African voting cohesion in the UN. Dorothy Dodge.

Africa Report. 12:67-70. O. '67. Africa in 240 minutes. E. S. Munger.

African Forum. 2:17-33. Winter '67. Must we lose Zimbabwe? T. M. Franck.

African Forum. 2:34-42. Winter '67. Nationalist movement in Zimbabwe. N. M. Shamuyarira.

African Forum. 2:43-9. Winter '67. Crisis in Rhodesia. Kotsho Dube.

African Forum. 2:50-65. Winter '67. Zambia in the aftermath of Rhodesian UDI: logistical and economic problems. F. T. Ostrander.

African Forum. 2:66-73. Winter '67. Colonialism and after: the political literature of Central Africa—a bibliographic essay. R. I. Rotberg.

African Forum. 2:87-97. Winter '67. East Africa vignettes. E. C. Fax.

America. 114:773-5. My. 28, '66. Russian revisionism in Africa. John O'Connor.

America. 114:867-8. Je. 25, '66. Inner black and white. Joseph Grosjean.

American History Review. 71:875-92. Ap. '66. Great Britain and the African peace settlement of 1919. W. R. Louis.

Annals of the American Academy of Political and Social Science. 372:93-104. Jl. '67. Africa and the world; nonalignment reconsidered; address, April 1967, with questions and answers. F. L. Hadsel.

Atlantic. 217:34+. F. '66. Atlantic report.

Atlantic. 218:128-31. Jl. '66. Up Kilimanjaro. G. M. Orenstein.

*Atlantic. 219:32-4+. Je. '67. Atlantic report: Tanzania.

Bulletin of the Atomic Scientists. 22:23-6. Ap. '66. Flow of ideas between Africa and America. W. S. Dillon.

*Bulletin of the Atomic Scientists. 22:19-21. O. '66. Developing the academic spirit in East Africa. D. P. S. Wasawo.

Business Week. p 126-7. My. 7, '66. Teaching the Kenyans to take a letter; secretarial training sponsored by ILO.

Business Week. p 151. N. 12, '66. New troubles hit African copper; trade boycott of Rhodesia reduces output in Zambia.

Business Week. p 34-5. Ja. 7, '67. Why the free world hungers for copper; production in Africa and Latin America hampered by racial conflict, political squabbles, and strikes.

*Business Week. p 108+. S. 2, '67. Business makes a Kenya safari.

Catholic World. 203:220-3+. Jl. '66. On misunderstanding Africa. John Lucal.

Catholic World. 205:358-64. S. '67. Africa's need: African socialism. John O'Connor.

Christian Century. 84:414. Mr. 29, '67. Communicating the word in Tanzania. W. B. Gray.

Christian Century. 84:512. Ap. 19, '67. Tanzania's brand of socialism pleases. E. A. Hawley.

*Christian Science Monitor. p 9. Ag. 19, '67. No rest for the Congo. A. H. House.

*Christian Science Monitor. p 5. O. 16, '67. Congolese struggle to regain balance. A. H. House.

Current History. 46:136-41+. Mr. '64. Tanganyika's two years of independence. Lionel Cliffe.

Current History. 46:142-7. Mr. '64. "Harambee" in Kenya. Colin Legum.

Current History. 46:148-55+. Mr. '64. Rhodesias and Nyasaland. F. M. G. Willson.

Current History. 46:156-62. Mr. '64. Somali Republic. Saadia Touval.

Current History. 46:163-8+. Mr. '64. Malagasy: patterns and prospects. W. J. Foltz.

Current History. 46:169-74. Mr. '64. Uganda: the politics of compromise. T. K. Hopkins.

Current History. 48:193-200+. Ap. '65. Organization of African unity. Arnold Rivkin.

Current History. 48:201-6+. Ap. '65. Zambia and Rhodesia: a study in contrast. Richard Brown.

Current History. 48:213-18+. Ap. '65. Rebellion in the Congo. M. D. Markowitz and H. F. Weiss.

Current History. 48:219-23+. Ap. '65. Tanzania: myth and reality. Lionel Cliffe.

Current History. 50:147-52. Mr. '66. East Africa, unity and diversity. L. Cliffe.

Current History. 51:20-7. Jl. '66. U.S. aid in Africa. Darrell Randall.

*Current History. 52:129-35+. Mr. '67. Africa in the world arena. K. W. Grundy.

Current History. 52:162-7+. Mr. '67. Prospects in Rhodesia. Richard Brown.

Current History. 52:168-74. Mr. '67. Confrontation in the Congo. Edouard Bustin.

Current History. 54:78-82+. F. '68. Ethiopia: the quickening pulse. W. H. Lewis.

Current History. 54:90-4+. F. '68. Nationalism and separatism in East Africa. K. W. Grundy.

Daedalus. 96:483-95. Spring '67. Color and power in the South African situation. Colin Legum.

Department of State Bulletin. 54:783. My. 16, '66. U.S. airlift to Zambia ends.

*Department of State Bulletin. 56:954-9. Je. 26, '67. America and Africa, the new world and the newer world; address at Haile Selassie I University in Addis Ababa, Ethiopia, May 26, 1967. N. deB. Katzenbach.
   Same. Vital Speeches of the Day. 33:622-5. Ag. 1, '67.

Department of State Bulletin. 57:656-60. N. 13, '67. America's understanding of Africa; address, October 21, 1967. Joseph Palmer, 2d.

Ebony. 21:128-33. Mr. '66. Ethiopia's modern Pheidippides: Abebe Bikila.

Ebony. 21:100-2+. My. '66. Everyone's keen on Keino. C. E. Brown.

Focus. 16:1-6. F. '66. Kenya. D. N. McMaster.

Focus. 17:1-6. S. '66. Sudan. J. R. Randell.

Foreign Affairs. 44:373-86. Ap. '66. Rhodesia in the context of southern Africa. J. K. Nyerere.

Harper's Magazine. 225:55-61. S. '62. East Africa: the birth pangs of independence. E. R. F. Sheehan.

Harper's Magazine. 233:124+. N. '66. View from Africa. Clayton Fritchey.

Holiday. 39:38-47+. Je. '66. Zambia. Nadine Gordimer.

Life: 61:3. Ag. 5, '66. Our Eisie and Kenya's Kenyatta. G. P. Hunt.

Life. 61:36-49+. Ag. 5, '66. Kenyatta of Kenya; with report by Hugh Moffett.

Nation. 203:712-13. D. 26, '66. Return to the bush. E. T. Chase.

National Review. 18:569. Je. 14, '66. End of King Freddie. Elspeth Huxley.

National Review. 18:1222. N. 29, '66. Communist grab for African unions. L. M. Taubinger.

National Review. 19:507. My. 16, '67. UN: the grip loosens.

*Natural History. 75:8-10+. O. '66. Report from Africa: a people apart, Ik tribe. C. M. Turnbull.

Negro History Bulletin. 30:19-20. Ja. '67. Monthly report on Africa. Paul McStallworth.

Negro History Bulletin. 30:11. O. '67. Africa and slave trade in the classroom. W. L. Katz.

New Republic. 155:15-17. Ag. 27, '66. Old hand's new look at seventeen countries. R. W. Howe.

New Republic. 156:13-14. Ja. 28, '67. High cost of historic rights: what the Portuguese face in Africa. Philip Ben.

New Republic. 157:13-16. S. 16, '67. Plot and counter-plot: what happened in the Congo. Keith Kyle.

*New York Times. p 58. Ja. 27, '67. East Africa draws closer to Zambia.

New York Times. p 60. Ja. 27, '67. Uganda stressing increased domestic savings as key to revival of development.

*New York Times. p 25. F. 5, '67. Indians are upset in Eastern Africa. Lawrence Fellows.

*New York Times. p 8+. D. 2, '67. 3 East African nations inaugurate trade bloc. Lawrence Fellows.

New York Times. p 49+. Ja. 26, '68. Africa: spirit of self-help builds unity. Brendan Jones.

New York Times. p 58. Ja. 26, '68. Common market concept gains in Africa. Lawrence Fellows.

New York Times. p 58. Ja. 26, '68. Somalia pins hopes on peace.

New York Times. p 58. Ja. 26, '68. Tanzania on road to rural socialism.

New York Times. p 59+. Ja. 26, '68. Africa finds image of its past dies hard.

New York Times. p 60. Ja. 26, '68. Kenya's growth rate lags behind goal. Henry Reuter.

*New York Times. p 60. Ja. 26, '68. Uganda gain slow but sure.

New York Times. p 62. Ja. 26, '68. After 2 lean years, Ethiopia is thriving.

New York Times. p 66. Ja. 26, '68. Zambia strained by crises and curbs. John Leech.

New York Times. p 68. Ja. 26, '68. Malawi: new ties.

New York Times. p 1+. F. 28, '68. Commons, by a big vote, backs curb on immigration of Asians [from East Africa]. Anthony Lewis.

Newsweek. 70:45. Jl. 3, '67. King's story; President Obote decrees total abolition of Buganda.

Newsweek. 70:45. Ag. 7, '67. Tanzania: follow that car!

Newsweek. 70:46+. S. 11, '67. Kenya: *shifta* revolt.

Newsweek. 70:117+. N. 13, '67. East African holiday.

Outdoor Life. 139:48-51+. F. '67. Old Shuguli. Alice Landreth.

Reader's Digest. 88:119-23. Mr. '66. Metamorphosis of Jomo Kenyatta. C. T. Rowan.

Reporter. 34:37-9. Mr. 10, '66. Transformation of Jomo Kenyatta. Clyde Sanger.

Reporter. 37:41-3. Jl. 13, '67. Paving Tanzania's way with good intentions: the Arusha Declaration. Anthony Delius.

Reporter. 37:38-40. O. 5, '67. Africa's guerrillas extend their fight. Anthony Delius.

Saturday Review. 49:84-5+. D. 10, '66. Training for the journalist in Africa and Vietnam. John Tebbel.

Saturday Review. 49:30+. D. 31, '66. Maybe on Tuesdays. Alan Wykes.

Saturday Review. 50:59-60+. Ag. 19, '67. Hazards of educational planning. Remi Clignet.

Saturday Review. 50:41-2. S. 9, '67. African safari view of the U.N. S. S. Baker.

Saturday Review. 50:52+. S. 16, '67. Portugal in Africa: Angola and Mozambique. Alden Voth.

Science. 158:876-81. N. 17, '67. East Africa: science for development. T. R. Odhiambo.

Science News. 91:552-3. Je. 10, '67. Marine lab in East Africa: Kanduchi, Tanzania. Charles Weiss, Jr.

Science News. 92:141. Ag. 5, '67. African food survey. D. A. Ehrlich.

Senior Scholastic. 89:pt2 8-9. S. 23, '66. Profile of Africa: continent in search of identity.

Senior Scholastic. 91:8. O. 5, '67. Man, we've got enough problems of our own! S. Lewin.

Time. 87:39. F. 25, '66. Hell run.

Time. 87:28. Mr. 25, '66. Trouble with Odinga.

Time. 87:40. Ap. 8, '66. Sense at the summit: Nairobi.

Time. 87:40. Ap. 29, '66. Trouble for Kenyatta.

Time. 87:35-6. My. 6, '66. Smugglers of flesh: Kenya and Tanzania.

Time. 87:36. My. 13, '66. Sharper panga.

Time. 87:30+. Je. 3, '66. Battle of Mengo hill.

Time. 88:33. Jl. 8, '66. Another sweep for Jomo.

Time. 88:46. Jl. 15, '66. Toward a native press; Nairobi press institute.

Time. 88:29. S. 2, '66. Incident in Djibouti.

Time. 88:46. S. 30, '66. Costly choice.

Time. 89:32+. F. 24, '67. Black resentment for the Asians.

Time. 89:42. Je. 16, '67. Uncommon cry; East African Community created.

Time. 90:26. S. 8, '67. Success at pacification; Somali guerrillas in revolt.

Time. 90:38+. O. 13, '67. Tough shepherd; new constitution.

Time. 90:40. N. 24, '67. Dressing up the Masai.

Travel. 125:56-60. F. '66. Uganda. Olga Achtenhagen.

Travel. 128:30-5. N. '67. Easy adventure: East Africa. S. M. Howland.

U.S. News & World Report. 60:69-71. Ja. 31, '66. How democracy is working out in black Africa.

U.S. News & World Report. 60:82-3. F. 14, '66. Whites in Kenya: what's their fate? A. J. Meyers.

*U.S. News & World Report. 63:56. O. 23, '67. Africa's "hidden" race war.

UNESCO Courier. 19:11-15. Ja. '66. New patterns of transport for Africa. W. H. Owens.

UNESCO Courier. 20:27-9. Ap. '67. Orphanage for wild animals. Richard Greenough.

UNESCO Courier. 20:4-8+. Je. '67. Birth of a new Africa. Gabriel d'Arboussier.

UNESCO Courier. 20:33-6. Je. '67. Today's schools prepare tomorrow's African scientists. N. C. Otieno.

United Nations Monthly Chronicle. 3:59-64. F. '66. First steps in a development project; development of the Pangani and Wami River basins; irrigated farming.

United Nations Monthly Chronicle. 3:53-4. My. '66. Promotion of African trade; summary of five-day meeting of African experts, Addis Ababa.

United Nations Monthly Chronicle. 4:27. F. '67. ECA conference in industry and finance.

United Nations Monthly Chronicle. 4:18. Ap. '67. Southern Rhodesia: Report of the Secretary-General.

Vogue. 149:146-7+. Ap. 1, '67. Africa: safari. Candice Bergen.

DATE DUE

GAYLORD

PRINTED IN U.S.A.